General Synod   GS Misc 198

D1646004

The Ordination of Woi.
to the Priesthood:
Further Report

A background paper by

Christian Howard

ISBN 0 7151 3699 2

CIO PUBLISHING
Church House, Dean's Yard, London SW1P 3NZ

PREFACE

This is the third in a series of reports on the Ordination of Women for which I have had the privilege to be responsible. The original consultative document (GS 104) was published in 1972 and a supplementary report (GS Misc 88) in 1978, in each case to assist the General Synod with consideration of this matter. This present report presupposes access to the earlier ones, since the historical introduction and the chapters on the Anglican Communion and the Ecumenical Evidence are largely concerned with events and material since 1978.

In addition, much of the material in Chapters II, VI and VII is written on the assumption that the reader will also take into account the central part of GS 104, on the biblical evidence, tradition and theological questions.

Anyone reading the three reports will see that they differ in style. GS 104, though it contains quotations from published material, is largely my own summary and survey of the whole range of views then current on the ordination of women. GS Misc 88 was almost wholly concerned with an updating of the Historical Preface, and of the Anglican Communion and Ecumenical Evidence. When I was asked to prepare this further report, it seemed to me, and to those whom I consulted, that, twelve years later, reflection was needed on those issues which may have newly emerged or which have received fresh emphasis. After more than a decade of debate, there is a considerable amount of published material and perhaps a clearer picture as to which issues are now of particular concern. Therefore, in addition to a further updating of the historical, Anglican Communion and ecumenical information, I have attempted to survery the issues as they are currently expressed, but on this occasion by extensive quotation from published (and occasionally unpublished) material. I hope this may be of service to the Synod.

Preparation of this report would have been impossible without much help from many people, and to these I express my warmest thanks. In particular, first of all to the three consultants appointed to advise me: the Bishop of Salisbury, Canon Colin Buchanan and Canon Roger Greenacre. For information on the Anglican Communion and the ecumenical situation: Canon Colin Craston and Mr John Martin (ACC), Canon Christopher Hill (Archbishop's Assistant for Ecumenical Affairs), Canon Martin Reardon (Board for Mission and Unity), the Rev. Colin Davey (BCC), Mrs Frances Sheppard and the Rev. Alice Medcof (Canada), the Rev. Janet Crawford (New Zealand), the Rev. Sandra Boyd (USA), Komminister Kerstin

Berglund and Dr Gunnel Mellbin (Sweden), and the authorities of the Church of Scotland and the English Free Churches. Dr Gordon Wenham kindly provided me with his *Churchman* article and a personal letter of further comment. For information on women's ministry, I am grateful to Mr Douglas Fryer (Statistical Unit), Miss Andrea Mulkeem (ACCM) and the Diocesan Lay Ministry Advisers.

Dr John Stott most helpfully made available to me a chapter from his forthcoming book *Issues Facing Christians Today* and SPCK generously allowed me to see an advance copy of the typescript of *Feminine in the Church,* edited by Monica Furlong, both of which were very useful to me. I am particularly grateful to Miss Karen Smurthwaite for typing most of the report.

Finally, the person to whom I owe most, for without her this report could not have been completed, is Mary Tanner (BMU). She guided me to many useful sources of information and ideas, appraised the work at various stages, and has been a constant source of encouragement and support.

CHRISTIAN HOWARD

September 1984

List of Contents

Page

I HISTORICAL INTRODUCTION

1. GS 104, paras 1-15 set out the circumstances which gave rise to its preparation as a Consultative Document and to the debates which it was intended to serve. In GS Misc 88 (paras 11-30), the history was carried forward to the period immediately before the November 1978 debate in General Synod and elsewhere, and included Resolutions of the 1978 Lambeth Conference. In GS 104 and in GS Misc 88, details of the situation in the Anglican Communion and the ecumenical evidence were separately considered and this practice has been followed here.

The 1978 Debate

2. The origin of the 1978 debate lay in the motion in the name of Canon Craston carried in July 1975:

> That this Synod invites the House of Bishops, when, in the light of developments in the Anglican Communion generally as well as in this country, they judge the time for action to be right, to bring before the Synod a proposal to admit women to the priesthood.

3. The House of Bishops invited the Bishop of Birmingham (the Rt Rev. H.W. Montefiore) to bring the matter before General Synod in November 1978, and he moved the following motion:

> That this Synod asks the Standing Committee to prepare and bring forward legislation to remove the barriers to the ordination of women to the priesthood and their consecration to the episcopate.

4. The Standing Committee had arranged for the Bishop of Truro (the Rt Rev. G.D. Leonard) to be given equal time to oppose the motion and to be entitled both to comment on all amendments and to reply to the debate.

5. Canon J.M. Free (Bristol) moved as an amendment, to *add* at the end:

> In order that those vocations claimed by some women may be tested whether they be of God.

The amendment was lost.

6. Canon D.A. Rhymes (Southwark) moved as an amendment, to *add* at the end:

> but not to introduce a measure into the Synod for General Approval until a consensus of agreement with this decision has been reached with the Roman Catholic and Eastern Orthodox Churches after official theological dialogue on this matter as requested by the General Synod in 1975.

1

(This refers to the motion moved in 1975 by the Rev L.G. Moss and carried in an amended form: see GS Misc 88, paragraph 23).

The amendment was lost.

7. The Rev Professor D.R. Jones (Durham and Newcastle Universities) moved as an amendment to *add* at the end:

> but not to introduce a measure into the Synod for General Approval until the official dialogue with the Roman Catholic and Eastern Orthodox Churches, as requested in the General Synod in 1975, has taken place.

The amendment was lost.

8. After the Bishops of Truro and Birmingham had replied to the debate, the Synod divided on the main motion, which was *lost* in the House of Clergy.

There voted:

	Ayes	Noes
House of Bishops	32	17
House of Clergy	94	149
House of Laity	120	106
	Abstentions 3	

(For the debate, see the *Report of Proceedings* for November 1978, pp.996 -1070)

After the 1978 Debate

MR CHANDLER'S RESOLUTION ON THE ORDINATION OF WOMEN AND THE MINISTRY OF WOMEN

9. Two of the amendments in the 1978 debate were concerned with dialogue with the Roman Catholic and Eastern Orthodox Churches. While they had been received with considerable sympathy (the present Archbishop of Canterbury, then Bishop of St Albans, suggested tripartite conversations), it appeared that some who would have supported one or other of the amendments did not do so because they were amendments to the main motion rather than distinct motions. Immediately after the 1978 debate, therefore, Mr Maurice Chandler (Birmingham) put down a Private Member's Motion as follows:

> that the Presidents be invited, after consultation with the Standing Committee, to initiate official discussions with the Roman Catholic Church, the Orthodox Churches and such other episcopally ordered Churches as may be appropriate on the subjects of the Ordination of Women and the Ministry of Women.

2

10. In due course, this motion came up for debate in July 1980. Earlier in the same session, Canon Rhymes asked the Archbishop of Canterbury (as Chairman of the House of Bishops):

> In view of the statement made in the last Presidential Address of the previous Archbishop that as a result of conversations with Cardinal Hume regarding the Roman Catholic attitude to the ordination of women as a matter of faith or discipline the Cardinal had promised to take the matter up with the Pope and his advisers and that we awaited further word from him: (a) Has any such further word been received and what is the present state of such consultations with the Roman Catholic Church? (b) Will the Bishops, in consultation with the Standing Committee, initiate official discussions with the Roman Catholic Church, the Orthodox Churches and other episcopally ordered Churches on this subject?

The Archbishop of Canterbury:

> At this stage there is nothing which I can usefully add to the statement made by my predecessor except to assure Canon Rhymes that this matter has not been, and will not be, overlooked. On the second part of his question, I do not think that a formal official discussion on this subject with other Churches is yet possible. I can understand the wish of many members of the Synod to have this prominently on the Agenda soon, but they will recognise that this sense of urgency is not shared by many of those in these sister Churches with whom we are in dialogue.

> The way forward at present is perhaps to ensure that the subject is raised in the context of our general discussion on the nature of ministry.

(For the statement by the Archbishop of Canterbury, Dr F.D. Coggan, in February 1979, see *Report of Proceedings* pp.2, 3 and Appendix I).

11. Mr Chandler, noting that the debate had been overtaken by the Archbishop's answer to Canon Rhymes' question, nevertheless thought the matter worthy of Synodical debate.

Professor J.D. McClean (Sheffield) moved as an amendment:

> In line 3, *leave out* 'episcopally ordered'.

The amendment was lost.

Mr Chandler's motion was carried.

RELATED DEBATES

12. Three other issues which have been before General Synod since 1978, though not directly part of the question whether or not the Church of England should ordain women as priests, have nevertheless, in varying degrees, contributed to that debate: Women Ordained Abroad, the Proposals for a Covenant, and Women Deacons. (Draft Measures concerned with the first and third of these matters are currently before the Synod.)

3

Women Ordained Abroad

13. Before the 1978 Debate, the Standing Committee had announced its intention, if the Bishop of Birmingham's motion were not carried, to set up a group to consider the position of women lawfully ordained abroad who subsequently came to this country, and to identify the options open to the Church of England. Accordingly, the Standing Committee appointed a group from among its own members under the chairmanship of Professor J.D. McClean. The group consisted, in addition to the Chairman, of two members from each of the three Houses, together with the Dean of the Arches.

14. The group's report (GS 415) came before General Synod in July 1979. It listed seven options: option 1 proposed no action, options 2 and 3 no action for five years (for differing reasons), options 4 and 5 proposed a permanent Measure to enable women ordained abroad to minister in the Church of England, either on the same terms as men ordained abroad (4) or only in specified circumstances and for a limited period (5). Options 6 and 7 were similar to 4 and 5 save that the Measure itself would be a temporary one with a non-renewable life of five - seven years. (For fuller details and for legal opinions, etc. see GS 415 and Chapter VII.)

15. The debate was in two parts. First, Professor McClean (Sheffield) moved on behalf of the Standing Committee that the Report of the Group be received. After a short debate, Canon P.A. Welsby (Rochester), who had been a member of the group, moved:

> That this Synod asks the Standing Committee to prepare and introduce legislation as envisaged in Option 7 in paragraph 21 of GS 415.

(This option was for a temporary measure for women priests to minister in specified circumstances and for a limited period.)

16. Following the 1978 precedent, Mr Oswald Clark (Southwark) was given an equal opportunity with Canon Welsby to oppose the motion and to respond to the debate.

17. The motion was lost in the House of Clergy. There voted:

	Ayes	Noes
House of Bishops	26	10
House of Clergy	87	113
House of Laity	110	65

18. During the debate, reference was made to the effect that the vote might have on the proceedings of the Churches' Council for Covenanting (see next section), and it is somewhat ironical that, when Women Ordained Abroad

returned to the next General Synod in July 1982, it was debated on the day following the failure of the Covenant vote.

19. On that occasion, the matter came to the Synod as a Private Member's Motion in the name of Deaconess Diana McClatchey (Worcester):

That this Synod instructs the Standing Committee to introduce legislation based upon Option 5 in the Report *Women Lawfully Ordained Abroad* (GS 415) to enable women lawfully ordained to the priesthood in other Anglican provinces to be given permission to exercise their ministry on particular occasions during temporary visits to the Provinces of Canterbury and York.

(The distinction between Option 5 and Option 7, as moved in 1979 by Canon Welsby, is that Option 5 provides for a permanent and not a temporary measure.) The motion was carried. There voted:

	Ayes	*Noes*
House of Bishops	24	4
House of Clergy	106	68
House of Laity	103	60

20. The draft Women Ordained Abroad Measure was introduced for General Approval in November 1983. Prior to the debate, the Secretary-General informed the Synod that a petition had been received from 30 Synod members that the Measure be designated Article 8 business and that this had been considered by the Presidents, the Prolocutor of the Convocation of Canterbury, and the Chairman and Vice-Chairman of the House of Laity. They had decided that the Measure should be so designated on the ground that it proposed a permanent change in the Service of Holy Communion. The effect of this decision would be that it must be referred to Diocesan Synods and would require a two-thirds majority in each House of the General Synod at Final Approval stage.

21. When the Measure came before the July 1984 Synod, the Revision Committee had included in the Measure a provision which would have the effect of making it a Measure with a limited life. Since Article 8 relates to *permanent* changes, the Standing Committee had resolved (by 14 votes to 4) to remove the Article 8 designation.

22. The day before the Synod was due to debate the Revision stage of the Measure, the Archbishop of Canterbury made the following statement:

As Synod members know, more than 50 members have asked in recent days that under Article 8 (2) of the Constitution, the Presidents, Prolocutors and Chairman and Vice-Chairman of the House of Laity should reconsider the designation of the Women Ordained Abroad Measure.

It will be remembered that, following a similar application in November we resolved to designate the Measure as Article 8 business. It was then a permanent Measure. The Legal Adviser advised us that as a matter of law he considered that the Measure in its then permanent form was outside Article 8. We took careful account of that advice. But we felt that we had also to take account of the fact that the change which would be made was permanent and we considered that there would be a direct impact upon the service of Holy Communion. We accordingly decided, notwithstanding the legal advice, to designate the Measure as it then stood as Article 8 business. Our decision was taken by majority. The majority hold to the view that their decision was right.

On this occasion we had to consider a Measure no longer permanent, but temporary — in the sense that it would expire after seven years. We have met on two occasions and have spent more than three hours in discussion. The legal advice again is clear, namely that, on a strict legal construction, Article 8 does not apply. We had then to take account of the other element in our previous decision. We took due account of the fact that the Measure is temporary. But we had to recognise that in matters concerning ministry there is need for particular care. To admit a temporary change in our practice, such as the Measure provides, would mean the admission within our tradition irreversibly of a principle which the Synod has yet to write into Canon and Statute Law, namely, that a woman can carry out priestly functions in the Church of England. This consideration has led us, again by majority, to the judgement that the Measure in its now temporary form ought to be designated as Article 8 business.

A debate took place on the Revision stage but no amendments were moved. The Measure was passed and now goes to the dioceses for approval.

Proposals for a Covenant

23. It was recognised during the 1979 debate on Woman Lawfully Ordained Abroad that this vote seriously affected the work of the Churches' Council for Covenanting (see previous section). That Council first met a few weeks after the 1978 Synod debate and there were those, both within the Free Churches and the Church of England, who wondered whether the negative vote had doomed the Council's deliberations from the start. At its first meeting the Free Churches made it clear that they could not contemplate a division within their ministry such as would follow from the recognition of their male ministers alone, though they saw a possible way through by the use of a conscience clause. On the Anglican side it was felt that the recently appointed McClean group on Women Lawfully Ordained Abroad might produce relevant material and it was noted that four of the nine Anglican CCC members were members of that group.

24. The residential session of CCC held shortly after the 1979 decision not to allow Women Lawfully Ordained Abroad to officiate in this country, has been accurately described in *The Failure of the English Covenant* as the 'first crisis'. The officers of the Council — Bishop Kenneth Woollcombe (Chairman) and Mr Phillip Capper (Secretary) — described it as follows:

Many members came to the meeting feeling that the decision had closed the door to the recognition under a covenant of the women ministers of the English Free Churches, and one of them, the Rev. Professor D.R. Jones, announced his intention to resign. After a great deal of discussion we were led to believe that a distinction would be drawn between the situation created by the decisions of the General Synod with regard to the ordination of women and the reception of Anglican clergy from abroad, and the different situation which would arise under the Covenant which would require the Church of England to recognise the women ministers of the other Covenanting Churches. In a complicated Press Statement which was agreed sentence by sentence, the Anglican delegation declared *ex animo* that the recent decisions of the Church of England did not present an insuperable barrier to the Covenant. In the final vote on the whole Statement two of its members abstained. At that point, the Council made a decision of faith: it decided to continue its work, instead of pausing to consider the weight of Professor Jones' arguments against doing so. (*The Failure of the English Covenant,* 1982, pp.11, 12)

25.   The Anglican statement was as follows:

The Anglican group accepts that if the Church of England enters into Covenant with other Churches and the recognition of ministries is implemented according to Proposition 6, the act of covenanting itself will create a new situation in which all the ministers of the Covenanting Churches, men and women, will be incorporated into the presbyterate. We recognise, however, that there are Anglicans who would be unable to accept this situation and a conscience clause would need to be framed to meet their needs. We believe the Council should work out the implications of Propositions 6 and 7 for the continuing life of the Churches after Covenanting. We give our united support to this procedure, but it will be for the Synod eventually to decide whether the Church of England is willing to enter such a Covenant.

26.   The CCC itself therefore stated that:

all the ministries of the Covenanting Churches, men and women, will share together in reconciled ministries within the historic continuity of the ministry of the whole Church, it being recognised that a conscience clause will be required to meet particular needs of worshipping congregations and individuals. (Statement of 20th July, 1979)

(Quoted in *On behalf of the Covenant,* Statement by six Anglican Members, and reprinted in *Essays on the Covenant,* BCC, p.16)

27.   The Report of the Churches' Council for Covenanting, *Towards Visible Unity: Proposals for a Covenant,* 1980, said this:

5.4.2. The ministries so recognised and accepted will comprise all those men and women in the Covenanting Churches currently held by each of those Churches to be ordained to the ministry of the word and sacraments.

28. As this Report began to reach its final form, it became clear that three of the Anglican nine members would dissent from some of the proposals, including that on women ministers. In their Memorandum of Dissent, printed at the end of *Towards Visible Unity,* they state:

> In para.5.4.1. of Chapter 5 it is affirmed that 'In the national Covenant Service the covenanting churches recognise and accept the ministries of all the covenanting churches as true ministries of the Gospel within the One, Holy, Catholic and Apostolic Church . . . ' and para.5.4.2. makes plain that 'the ministries so recognised and accepted will comprise all those men and women in the covenanting churches currently held by each of those churches to be ordained to the ministry of the Word and Sacraments.' Para.5.4.3. adds that the ministries of *all* the covenanting churches 'must be so ordered that they are seen to have the authority not of one church only but of *all* the covenanting churches.' It is obvious that the requirements of paras.5.4.2. and 5.4.3. in the unqualified form in which they now stand present grave difficulty for the Church of England. (*Towards Visible Unity,* p.90, paragraph 27)

This difficulty is further spelled out in the following paragraphs (28-35).

29. But what of the rights of conscience, referred to by a leading Free Churchman at the first meeting? Within the two year period prescribed for finishing the Report (a deadline laid down by the General Synod in 1978) the CCC only had time to produce a chapter of five paragraphs which its officers were later to describe as 'inadequate' and added: 'Certainly it did not allay the fears of many in the Churches' debates who were concerned about rights of conscience' (*Failure of the English Covenant,* p.16). The nub of the problem was summed up in the Proposals as follows:

> The act of Covenanting will not of itself require bishops and other ministers or members to act in conflict with their personal convictions. All however in exercising their right of personal conviction must seek to act so that the substance of the Covenant is not negated. (*Towards Visible Unity,* p.64, para.7.1)

30. Two things must be added: first, though Anglicans tended to see rights of conscience primarily in terms of the right not to receive the ministry of women ministers, (or indeed the ministry of any non-episcopally ordained ministers), Free Churchmen, particularly in the United Reformed Church, were concerned about other rights of conscience. Secondly, since the Proposals were concerned not so much with matters concerning internal Church matters but the relationship between Churches, the assumption was that:

> Such rights and reservations shall in the first instance be upheld by the pastoral practices of the Church concerned. It shall be for the Churches acting together through the collegiality of the local episcopate and of national leadership to determine when these rights and reservations are asserted to the injury of their developing unity and peace, or so as to negate the substance of the Covenant.(*Towards Visible Unity* p.64, para.7.4)

Clearly this was not enough for the dissentients and, in particular, they held that:

insufficient attention has been paid to the conscience of a bishop *qua* bishop and also to what may not unfairly be regarded as the conscience of a particular Church. (*Towards Visible Unity*, p.93, para.37)

31. After the publication of its Report, the CCC continued its work, and set up a Working Group on 'Conscience, with particular reference to Women's Ordination'. An extract from its careful report is to be found in Appendix II of *The Failure of the English Covenant*. (For its section on the meaning of 'conscientious reservation' see Appended Note 1, A Conscience Clause, p.53 below.)

32. In February 1981, the Board for Mission and Unity brought to the Synod its Report on the Proposals (*The Covenant — an Assessment*, GS 473), and after a short debate this was received. The crucial motion which followed, recognised that acceptance of women ministers was one of the three key questions. It was moved in the following form by the Bishop of Guildford:

That this Synod believing that the Proposals entitled 'Towards Visible Unity: Proposals for a Covenant' are the appropriate step towards visible unity for the Church of England, accepts:
(a) its provisions concerning existing Provincial Moderators of the United Reformed Church;
(b) its provisions for the reconciliation of Churches incorporating their ministries within the historic ministry of the catholic Church;
(c) its provisions for the recognition and acceptance of women ministers of the other Covenanting Churches as presbyters.

33. At the end of the debate each part of the motion was put separately and the voting on (c) was as follows:

	Ayes	Noes
Bishops	37	9
Clergy	144	89
Laity	166	66

Clause (c) of the motion had marginally the highest negative vote. The Proposals as a whole then received Provisional Approval. When the debate on Final Approval took place in July 1982, the vote failed in the House of Clergy to reach the two-thirds majority required in each House. Since the vote was simply on a motion to give Final Approval it is not possible to distinguish which of the various issues led to its failure, though the proposals for reconciliation of ministries and the need to accept women ministers both seem to have been major questions.

Deacons (Ordination of Women) Measure
34. In November 1981, the House of Bishops brought to the Synod a Report on *The Deaconess Order and the Diaconate* (GS 506), the purpose of which is clearly stated in the first paragraph:

1. The House of Bishops undertook to consider Resolution 20 of the 1978 Lambeth Conference, which was in the following terms:

   'The Conference recommends, in accordance with Resolution 32(c) of the Lambeth Conference of 1968, those member Churches which do not at present ordain women as deacons now to consider making the necessary legal and liturgical changes to enable them to do so, instead of admitting them to a separate order of deaconesses'.

The Bishops had asked ACCM to prepare a background paper, and this was annexed to the Report. It went on to say:

3. In the course of its consideration of these matters, the House has also taken into consideration the recommendation of the 1968 Lambeth Conference to the effect that all those already duly made deaconess should be declared to be within the diaconate.

4. The House considers that it is desirable that the General Synod should now indicate whether it considers that there should be a single order of deacons, open to both men and women. The House of Bishops for its part is in favour of this.

5. If the Synod desires to see a single diaconal order, thought must then be given to the steps by which this may be achieved. One possibility would be to act upon the 1968 Lambeth Conference resolution, with a simple declaration that all those already duly admitted to the deaconess order are regarded within the diaconate, followed by the necessary legislation to give effect to it. It would necessarily follow that all further ordinations would be to the order of deacons. Another possibility is to provide that future ordinations of both men and women should be to the order of deacons, with provision being made for the admission to the order of deacons of any existing deaconess who desires this.

6. The House of Bishops had invited the Bishop of Portsmouth to test opinion on the proposition that future ordinations of men and women should be to a single diaconal order, with provision being made for the admission to that order of existing deaconesses who so desire. If this motion is carried, there will have to be legislation to give effect to it.

The Report also suggested that consideration of the principle should not be confused by discussion as to how the members of the single diaconal order should be represented synodically.

35. Two matters were to complicate subsequent debates. (i) In July 1981, Mr T.L. Dye (York) had successfully moved a Private Member's Motion:

That this Synod requests the House of Bishops to consider ways in which the

Diaconate can once more become a vital and active element in the threefold Ministry in the Church of England, and bring to this Synod practical proposals, in particular consideration of the following possibilities is requested:

(i) That it should be a ministry open to men and women on a lifelong basis, in addition to its present use as a probationary period before Ordination to the Priesthood;

(ii) Any proposals brought forward should not be in a form which in any way prejudges questions relating to the Ordination of Women to the Priesthood;

(iii) That selection for this Ministry, and training for it, need not be in the same form as that adopted for the Priesthood.

This motion was not intended to raise a debate on women in the diaconate, but rather to seek a more far reaching consideration of what has come to be called 'a distinctive diaconate'. The House of Bishops' proposals were concerned, as their Report shows, with a more limited aim: namely to try and deal with the anomalies in the position of the deaconess. However, with Mr Dye's motion duly carried, a number of members in the November debate (and subsequently), felt it inopportune to proceed further with admitting women to the existing diaconate before the far reaching consideration for which that motion had asked had taken place. (The future course of the work for which Mr Dye asked, passed to ACCM and was subsumed into the Tiller Report.)

(ii) At the stage when it brought its Report to the Synod, the House of Bishops had not apparently made up its mind on how existing deaconesses should become deacons. One result was the lengthy time taken by the Working Party of the Standing Committee which prepared the legislation, and the prolonged debates on this matter in the Synod.

36. In November 1981, the major debate took place on the Bishop of Portsmouth's motion to receive the Report (GS 506). This was carried, and the Bishop then moved:

That this Synod, believing that within the historic threefold ministry the Order of Deacons is an order open to women asks the Standing Committee to prepare legislation to ensure that, from a future date, all candidates — both men and women — sponsored for diaconal service should be admitted to the Order of Deacons and to make provision for the admission to the Order of Deacons of those previously admitted to the Order of Deaconesses who so desire.

The Bishops indicated that the House of Bishops had preferred the second of the two possibilities in paragraph 5 of GS 506 because simply to declare deaconesses 'to be within the diaconate' would make no allowance for any deaconesses who did not wish to be so declared. He also made it clear that, once bishops were authorised to ordain women as deacons, there would be no further admissions to the Order of Deaconess.

37. Three somewhat similar amendments were moved by Dr Wright

Holmes, Dr Bennett and Mr Dye and were all lost. The amendment moved by Dr G.V. Bennett (Oxford University) was:

> *Delete* all words after 'That this Synod' and *insert* 'While affirming that there are no fundamental objections to the ordination of women to the historic Order of Deacons, requests the House of Bishops to enlarge its consideration of the place of the Diaconate in the Church's Ministry in accordance with Mr T.L. Dye's motion passed in July 1981, and to bring forward proposals for the admission of Deaconesses and others (both men and women) to the Order of Deacons in such a way that there may be a distinctive and permanent Diaconate in the Church of England'.

The Rev. B.D.T. Brindley (Oxford) then moved:

> Add at end:
> 'but not to take action unless, in the judgement of the Standing Committee, it seems likely from the voting figures on this motion that the necessary legislation could be carried through all stages with the requisite majorities in all three Houses of the Synod.'

The amendment was lost.
The Bishop of Portsmouth's motion was carried.

38. In November 1982, the Synod debated: *The Ordination of Women to the Diaconate: Report by the Standing Committee* (GS 549). This described the legislation proposed to enable women to become deacons and how existing deaconesses were to become deacons. Most of this was uncontroversial but the main difficulty had arisen over proposals concerning existing deaconesses. The Standing Committee Report had opted for 'conditional ordination'. In introducing the Report, Mr Smallwood drew attention to discussion of this matter in the House of Bishops who had voted 35 to 2 in favour of the use of conditional ordination in the case of existing deaconesses but of ordination *ab initio* for all new cases.

39. The Synod then voted for the introduction of legislation along the lines of the Report:

	Ayes	*Noes*
House of Bishops	35	1
House of Clergy	120	63
House of Laity	127	53

40. In July 1983, the legislation was finally introduced (GS 580) but was accompanied by a Report from the Standing Committee (GS 580A) suggesting that, notwithstanding the provision in the draft Measure that a deaconess may be conditionally ordained deacon, the Standing Committee considered on reflection that Archdeacon Silk's suggestion of 'supplemental ordination' would be the course to adopt. This Report also contained two schedules giving model liturgical forms of service for ordaining existing

deaconesses as deacon, in the style of the BCP Ordinal and in that of the ASB.

41. The expression 'supplemental ordination' was heavily criticised in the debate, and Archdeacon Silk's motion on this was amended to read:

That this Synod welcomes the model liturgical forms in Schedules I and II to the Report and, subject to the draft Measure being given General Approval, instructs the Revision Committee, in revising the Measure, to enable liturgical forms based on these models to be used.

After this motion was carried, the Synod debated the General Approval motion which was carried. There voted:

	Ayes	Noes
House of Bishops	28	0
House of Clergy	118	33
House of Laity	111	33
	Abstentions 2	

42. When the draft Measure returned to the Synod in February 1984, it had been radically altered by the Revision Committee, who had decided that the appropriate legislation would be a short enabling Measure accompanied by a Canon. The Measure therefore permits the making of provision by Canon for the ordination of women as deacons, but makes it explicitly clear that nothing in the Measure makes it lawful 'for a woman to be ordained to the office of a priest'. Synod may also by Canon provide that no woman shall be admitted to the order of deaconess after the date on which the Measure comes into force unless she had already been accepted for training for that order. However nothing in the measure would affect the rights of a deaconess who does not become a deacon. The Measure also deals with pension matters.

43. The most controversial proposal concerned the matter of representation in the General Synod. It had originally been hoped that the legislation would be completed and the first women made deacons in time for them to stand for the House of Clergy in the 1985 General Synod election, (the Election 80 Group having decided that no special representation of deacons should be provided for). When it became clear that the timetable would not allow for this, the Revision Committee had provided, by Clause and Schedule, an amendment to the Church Representation Rules so that a deaconess elected to the House of Laity of diocesan or General Synod in 1985, and subsequently ordained deacon, would not lose her seat until 1988 (diocesan synod) or 1990 (General Synod). This was unacceptable to the Standing Committees of the Houses of Clergy and Laity, and Canon Boulton and Mr Oswald Clark successfully proposed in its place an amendment to Canon H2

(concerning representation of Clergy in Convocations) which would enable a special constituency of voters for women deacons, divided according to their numbers between Canterbury and York, to elect a proportionate number of their members to the Convocations. The date of this election would be fixed by the Presidents and the members would sit until 1990, after which this special constituency would disappear. The Revision stage of the Measure was completed and Canon C4A 'Of Women Deacons' and Amending Canon No. 12 were both generally approved and revised in full Synod.

44. The Measure is now referred to diocesan synods for approval.

II THE PRESENT STATE OF THE DEBATE

Arguments that are currently used

45. Before considering the theological and other arguments that are most frequently heard, it is salutary to reflect on a paragraph by the Orthodox theologian Thomas Hopko in 'Women and the Priesthood: Reflections on the Debate' (*Women and the Priesthood,* ed. T. Hopko, St Vladimir's Seminary 1983).

> When reading books and articles on the subject of the ordination of women, including the works referred to here, one quickly becomes convinced that virtually everyone enters this debate with a conviction about the truth of the matter and what ought to be done about it. The 'material' of the debate — scriptural texts, patristic treatises, conciliar decrees, canonical laws, historical events — are interpreted in the light of this conviction, and the arguments for or against the ordination of women are presented accordingly, using the sources to defend that position. This does not mean that those involved in the debate are dishonest and prejudiced, but rather that they are, quite understandably and naturally, formed by a tradition that provides and shapes their general vision of things. This general vision results from a combination of theological, moral, liturgical, ecclesial, social and cultural experiences that come together to produce a basic 'feeling' and 'intuition' about the way things are and ought to be, in the light of which one interprets the words and actions of others, especially those of the past, including those ascribed to God in the Bible. . .
>
> What we want to affirm now is our conviction that no one really thinks, decides, and acts on the issue of women and the priesthood (or, for that matter, on any other issue) in a vacuum. Everyone does so from within a living tradition, in a lived situation and vital context. No one comes to the ''data'' of the debate in a thoroughly detached and disinterested manner. (pp.170-171)

Whatever our position, we all need to begin our current exploration by honestly recognising the truth of this comment, for only so can we appreciate the position of others, even when we remain in disagreement with them.

46. One such position is expressed by a correspondent thus:

> The question of the Ordination of Women to the Priesthood clearly raises theological issues which involve a major and fundamental alteration in what has been accepted by the church from the beginning as regards the subject of Ordination. Without entering into the merits or demerits of the various arguments about the theological issues, it seems to me beyond question that there are raised some fundamental questions and, therefore, the problem is how can these be properly settled. My own view is that this is a matter in which truth and unity are inseparable. It is not merely that individual parts of Christendom ought not to make practical decisions by themselves, but that the existence of disunity impairs

15

the theological judgement in the matter and I would argue that this could apply to the Roman Catholic and Orthodox Churches as well as to other Churches. So then it is not just a matter of Christian Unity, but a matter of how the right theological decision is to be arrived at which must be done clearly before any practical steps are taken. In the present state of divided Christendom it is not easy to be at all precise about the way in which this would be done, but I should have thought that even in advance of actual organisational union, or the acceptance of ecumenical decision-making bodies, it should be possible to discern the formation of a consensus in the matter one way or the other.

47. Two distinct questions are raised here:
(i) does the ordination of women involve a fundamental change?
(ii) how are decisions about fundamental change to be made?

DOES THE ORDINATION OF WOMEN INVOLVE A FUNDAMENTAL CHANGE?

48. The following quotation from the Roman Catholic *Declaration on the Question of the Admission of Women to Ministerial Priesthood (Inter insigniores)* illustrates the view that such action would indeed involve a fundamental change:

> In the final analysis it is the Church, through the voice of her Magisterium, that, in these various domains, decides what can change and what must remain immutable. When she judges that she cannot accept certain changes, it is because she knows that she is bound by Christ's manner of acting. Her attitude, despite appearances, is therefore not one of archaism but of fidelity: it can be truly understood only in this light. The Church makes pronouncements in virtue of the Lord's promise and the presence of the Holy Spirit, in order to proclaim better the mystery of Christ and to safeguard and manifest the whole of its rich content.

> This practice of the Church therefore has a normative character: in the fact of conferring priestly ordination only on men, it is a question of an unbroken tradition throughout the history of the Church, universal in the East and in the West, and alert to repress abuses immediately. This norm, based on Christ's example, has been and is still observed because it is considered to conform to God's plan for his Church. (Section 4)

49. On the other hand, the view that the ordination of women to the priesthood does not involve a fundamental change was expressed by Professor John Macquarrie when he addressed the 1978 Lambeth Conference:

> First of all, I think we have to get the problem into perspective. Most theologians would agree that in Christianity there is what has come to be called a hierarchy of truths, that is to say, there are some central doctrines which comprise the very heart of Christian faith, there are others which may be less central but are nevertheless moderately important and well attested, while there are others still which are more peripheral and about which there is some question as to whether or not they are implicates of the central truths. It seems to me quite clear that the

16

question of whether women can be priests belongs to this outer grey peripheral area. It is certainly not I would say a question by which Christian faith either stands or falls. (*Report of Lambeth Conference 1978*, p.118)

50. To sum up: on the one hand, though there is a readiness to be open to the possibility that women might be ordained, it is assumed by some that, since this would be contrary to the received practice of the Universal Church it would not be right to alter it without a clear and morally unanimous consensus of the whole body of Catholic Christendom. Those who argue in this way often appeal to 'the Catholic doctrine of Priesthood' which they see themselves as holding, not so much as a part of a minority in the Church of England, but rather as part of that great majority of Catholic Christendom, stretching from Anglicanism through the Roman Catholic and Orthodox Churches. For many such, priesthood is *essentially* male and must always be so. To quote Father Hopko again: 'to be father and husband in and to an ecclesial community is a masculine spiritual activity, that a woman, by nature and vocation, cannot and should not be expected to fulfil. . . . No woman is ever called to this vocation — her very womanhood precludes it, since she cannot possibly be a husband and father.' (Ibid, p.186) (See also Chapter VII) On the other hand, the question is raised by others how far details of Church Order are really theological, and, if they are, which details? Consideration of this inevitably involves discussion of the nature of biblical authority, the normative character of tradition and indeed the nature of men and women. It becomes increasingly clear that the debate about the ordination of women often turns on some previous question, on some fundamental assumptions about God or humankind, assumptions, furthermore, on which there are profound disagreements *within* the Church of England. (See Chapter VI)

HOW ARE DECISIONS ABOUT FUNDAMENTAL CHANGE TO BE MADE?

51. Father Hopko writes: 'The issue at hand. . . . is not one of change as such. It is rather of identifying how and in which ways the Church changes in order to remain truly herself.' (Ibid, p.174). This inevitably raises those previous questions mentioned above. But this whole matter also becomes involved with the argument, previously referred to: what agreement is needed and with whom, before it would be proper for the Church of England to ordain women? The ecumenical-authority argument is seen by many not as a practical matter but rather as a fundamental theological one, touching on the nature of the Church. It would be a matter of debate among Anglicans how far Article 34 (Of the Traditions of the Church) would apply. (See also Chapter VI)

52. Alongside the theological consideration of change, two further objections of a more pragmatic nature need to be noted. (These seem to have

had particular influence at the time of the 1978 debate in the General Synod.)

Anxiety lest action by the Church of England might prejudice the hoped for unity with the Roman Catholic Church.

53. This is to be distinguished from the theological ecumenical-authority argument, since it is sometimes persuasive for those who would, on other grounds, not object to the ordination of women. However, such a pragmatic position hardly takes account of the fact that the Church of England is only part of the Anglican Communion and that ARCIC is a conversation with that Communion and not the Church of England on its own. (See also Chapters V and VI)

54. Some would argue in reply (i) that Rome's dialogue with a Communion which as a world wide Communion has not yet pronounced formally one way or the other on the issue is on a very different footing from a dialogue with a Communion that has committed itself definitively and formally to the principle of women priests: (ii) that (rightly or wrongly) Rome attaches particular significance to the Church of *England,* and (iii) that those engaged in the ARCIC enterprise recognise that though the dialogue is between two world wide communions yet the process of reconciliation between them is likely to involve not only "unity by stages" but the possibility (at least) that in some parts of the world there may be a readiness to move ahead into one of these stages without waiting for a similar degree of preparedness in all other parts of the world.

Anxiety lest the issue prove intolerably divisive within the Church of England.

55. This argument appears to have weighed heavily with many lay members of Synod in 1978 and it surfaced again in the debates on the Covenant. On the other hand, it seems probable that one widespread view in favour of the ordination of women is simply that it is an idea whose time has come. On this view, women priests are the appropriate next step for the Church of England to take, and the experience of meeting women priests from other parts of the Anglican Communion has tended to reinforce this conviction in the minds of many people. Those who hold such a view tend to be impatient with the arguments of the opponents and not much concerned with many of the arguments in favour.

56. So far our consideration has been on the approach to the debate, on the parameters within which it is to be conducted, rather than on the specific issues themselves. These specific issues were substantially considered in GS 104, chapters IV-VII. The important question now is to ask whether, twelve years later, there are new issues to be taken into consideration. Whether or not there are fresh issues, or merely changes in the emphasis given to some of

them, it does appear that further reflection is needed both on some general issues, such as Ministry and Priesthood, Authority in the Church and the way decisions are made, and also on others which bear directly on the question of the ordination of women: the biblical conception of headship as applied to men and women in Church and Society, our understanding of the nature of God as it affects such arguments that the masculinity of God requires a male order of ministry, and arguments derived from the picture of the priest as the icon of Christ.

57. Before turning to a detailed consideration of new material and argument, it is important to reflect further on the way we do theology, since this affects our approach to the whole debate.

Doing Theology

58. What is meant by *doing* theology? Two recent reflections are perhaps worth quoting.

59. The first approach is what has sometimes been called the new hermeneutic, and has had a considerable effect, particularly in Evangelical circles. It is well set out by Dr Tony Thiselton in his preparatory paper for the 1977 National Evangelical Anglican Congress at Nottingham, entitled 'Understanding God's Word Today' (*Obeying Christ in a Changing World, The Lord Christ*, Collins, 1977). Quotations from his concluding theses may summarise his approach:

> The task of understanding the biblical text must include a careful investigation of its linguistic, historical, literary and theological context, and its setting in the ancient world. Often this may call for the use of resources provided by biblical scholarship. . . . Not only the ancient text but also the modern reader is conditioned by his place in history. . . . Historical distancing has a vital part to play in preventing premature 'applications'. It ensures that I do not only read my own ideas into the text. Understanding and appropriation depend, however, on a fusion between two sets of horizons, namely those of the text and those of the modern reader. Both distancing and fusion are equally necessary. The reader's own prior frame of reference both helps and hinders a right understanding of the text. He can begin only with his own questions; but these questions in turn, must be called in question by the text. Questioning one's own questions is a necessary part of biblical interpretation: understanding the biblical text is a process rather than an act. It involves both studying and listening, both careful reflection and response. The Bible not only conveys information to be learned, but also communicates God's word of address to be obeyed. . . . The Holy Spirit works through the kinds of means which have been set out above, and not usually in independence of them, even though this may sometimes occur. (pp.120-121)

60. A second reflection comes from Mary Tanner in 'Called to Priesthood: Interpreting Women's Experience' (*Feminine in the Church,* ed: Monica Furlong, SPCK, 1984):

The Holy Spirit in the midst of us and ahead of us is always challenging us to take a fresh look at what God has entrusted to His Church in Scripture and Tradition. It is in an interplay of Scripture and Tradition, Reason and Experience that we re-negotiate inherited doctrines and beliefs. This is what makes the Christian way very exciting, unexpected and always re-creative. In the dance between what we have inherited and what we experience, we as individuals and the Church as the Body of Christ, are led to new insights. Scripture sometimes marvellously confirms lived experience, says yes to what is new and radical. Equally we may not deny its power to judge and condemn our experience; it can and does sometimes say no to change.

This double dynamic process is being affirmed by more and more theologians who acknowledge that the experience of individuals and communities is a valid subject for reflection in theological endeavour. Careful attention to the way things function and the way things are is an essential part of 'doing theology'. They claim, with Bonhoeffer, the importance of 'never understanding the reality of God apart from the reality of the world'. God's word is heard, his demands perceived in a disturbing and creative inter-action between what is going on in the world and what has so far been understood, believed and practised in the Christian Tradition. This way of 'doing theology' is not new. It is the pattern described in contemporary biblical scholarship as the dynamic behind the canonical revelation. Prophets, Wisdom writers, Psalmists, Gospel writers, pondered on the traditions they had inherited in the light of their contemporary experience, both personal and national. With astonishing openness to the life-giving tradition, carried in their Scriptures and encountered in their worship, with openness to social and religious life and to personal relationships, above all, with an openness to the power of the Spirit, they were led to see new truths about the nature and being of God, to perceive new things about their relationship to God and to each other and were able to proclaim a vision for the present and immediate future. The Tradition passed on both within Scripture and outside is thus dynamic and not static. Development is part of the biblical and Christian way.

20

III THE CHANGED SITUATION IN ENGLAND

61. No debate on a real issue takes place in a vacuum: there is always a particular set of events, of common experience, a particular set of attitudes which are the setting within which the question is wrestled with. Other parts of this Report are concerned with the contexts of the General Synod, of the Anglican Communion, of ecumenism, and with the changes in those areas since 1978. In this section we are concerned with changes in the experience of women and in our understanding of ministry as the context within which the Church of England once again debates the ordination of women.

The Experience of Women

IN SOCIETY

62. What changes, have there been in the last ten to twelve years which may particularly affect women in this country?

The Sex Discrimination Act and the existence of the Equal Opportunities Commission together with the (earlier) Equal Pay Legislation have begun to improve the position of women in employment. However, the recession has almost certainly hit some working women hard, particularly perhaps married women who may work part time. For example a married woman teacher who may need to move jobs when her husband's employment means a change of home often now finds it impossible to be re-employed. Furthermore, the cry is once again heard that married women should stay at home and leave the jobs for the men. (If they no longer bother to register for work they will not now show up in the unemployment figures and it is difficult to know the size of the problem.)

63. The growing incidence of single parent families and women who are divorced or separated from their husbands (but not remarried) contributes further strains to the life experience of many women. How far have women reacted critically or in anger to these experiences? How far have men been blamed for women's distress? In general, it would appear, not very much but there has emerged a small but articulate women's movement (a term much to be preferred to the media-generated phrase, 'Women's Lib') particularly among younger women, often in touch with other radical movements. The women of the Greenham Common Peace Camp have undoubtedly drawn attention not only to the protest against Cruise Missiles but also to the potential strength of another style of protest.

64. So far as it concerns our particular question, it would seem that one of the aspects of the women's movement that is most likely to be influential is the attention it draws to the effect on women of role models in our society

which are all too often wholly male, not least in the area of ministry. An analogous situation arises when a girl in a co-educational school, contemplating teaching, experiences the disadvantages of all, or almost all, the senior posts being held by men. Another important aspect is the attention drawn to the effect on women of living and working within institutions and organisations operated by men and designed to fit their particular life style.

65. Christian feminists within (and outside) the Churches have the special task of interpreting the insights of the women's movement and 'women's stories' to other Christians. To listen to the stories and the experiences of women is to encounter *some* of the pain of our society — but a pain that is often too little recognised until attention is called to it.

IN THE CHURCH

66. Women make up a high proportion of most congregations: the experiences of women are varied and even contradictory, though perhaps, if we were making a list of them, we should add the voices of those women who, while calling themselves Christian, are, *because* of painful experiences, no longer in the congregation. How far have the churches attempted to come to grips with the experiences of women in society and in the Church, the pain and fustration — as well as, of course, the particular joys?

67. The WCC Study on the Community of Women and Men in the Church, culminating in the Sheffield Conference in 1981 (*Report,* WCC, 1983) has had its repercussions within British ecumenical and denominational structures. The BCC study group on the same theme has led in turn to the setting up of a group in the Church of England, one of whose tasks is to respond to the request for information as to what women are in fact doing in our Church, at every level. The report of this group, when it is published, will furnish important background material for our present debate. It might be claimed that at local level women are doing a great deal but *what*? Is there in fact a strongly marked division of tasks between men and women in our parishes, and if so, on what basis? Do women as well as men share in all the tasks? (This whole matter is inevitably also mixed up with the clerical/lay divide.) How far do the present patterns of church life have a 'selective' effect, i.e. drawing in those women who like a strongly marked role distinction between the sexes, and keeping out those who find it stifling?

68. If it is asked what all this has to do with the question of the ordination of women to priesthood, it must be said that the way the Church is experienced contributes towards forming that 'lived situation and vital context' to which Hopko refers and which is quoted in Chapter II and it is within this that church people come to conclusions and decisions on such matters as women priests.

69. The word *ministry* in its broadest sense denotes the service to which the whole people of God is called, whether as individuals, as a local community or as the Universal Church (*Baptism, Eucharist and Ministry, the Lima Text,* WCC Faith and Order Paper No.111, 1982 Statement on Ministry, p.21, para.7). Thus the practice of shared ministry among the whole people of God as we have experienced it increasingly in these last years is bound to provide more opportunities for women in the Church 'to discover the gifts they have received from God and to use them for the building up of the Church and for the service of the world to which the Church is sent' (Ibid. p.20, para.5).

70. Against this general but essential background of ministry, we now turn to consider the exercise of specific ministry by women, that of the accredited lay ministry (professionally trained, sometimes stipendiary, sometimes non-stipendiary) of deaconesses and licensed lay workers including Church Army Sisters. We consider this for two reasons: first, it is through the experience of the ministry of women that many people in fact come to their conviction about the ordination of women. This is not to suggest that seriously held theological convictions will always be overturned by experience. Nevertheless, for some at least, the interaction between experience and the tradition enables them to see their way forward, one way or the other: for some it amounts to knowing 'what it feels like'. The second reason for considering women's ministry is because of the effect that the experience of ministering has on the women themselves. In not a few cases, experience plus reflection on it, together with reflection on Bible and tradition, enables a woman to come to a clearer understanding. In some cases this may lead a woman to speak of a sense of call to priesthood.

71. What, then, are the changes that can be noted in the last decade? There appear to be three:
    (i)   a rise in the number of women offering for ministry
    (ii)   a very marked increase in deaconess ordinations
    (iii) some increase in posts of responsibility for women.

Women offering for ministry
72. For the last few years it has been common knowledge among those concerned for women's ministry that there has been this rise, and, furthermore, that the women coming forward are of a high calibre. One Archdeacon, after his first experience as a selector of women, announced bluntly that the women were abler than the men and this had finally led him to decide in favour of the ordination of women. However, when one tries to test out this rise in terms of statistics, it is more difficult to pinpoint the time it began or its exact size. For example, the total number of full-time women

workers (other than Church Army Sisters) fell from 363 in 1969 to 307 in 1976 and then began to rise. The total numbers, including part-time workers, remained steady until 1972 and then fell heavily until 1976, after which the total rose sharply. Part of the difficulty in making much of these statistics is that, between one year and another, women were not always counted in the same way, and, in any case, a different classification was introduced in 1982.

73. Total figures, however, do not tell us how many new entrants there were since we do not have the figures for retirements or of those leaving the work. A more reliable figure therefore might be that for candidates attending Selection Conferences. From 45 in 1973, this rose to 175 in 1983, nearly four times as many. However, if the figures for those Recommended and Conditionally Recommended are counted, they rise from 33 in 1973 to 102 in 1983. This is a much slower rate of rise than for attendances and there seems some evidence that the *proportion* of candidates Recommended for training is decreasing. Only since 1981 are the figures for candidates for Stipendiary and Non-Stipendiary Ministry shown separately. In the first two years the proportion of NSM candidates Recommended was slightly lower than for Stipendiary, but in 1983, when the proportion in both groups fell sharply, a lower proportion of the Stipendiary candidates (57 per cent) were Recommended than of the NSM (60 per cent).

74. The figures for women in training for Accredited Lay Ministry, show that in 1973 there were 58, a third of them training through non-residential courses. By 1983 this had risen to 218, of whom 116 were training non-residentially.

75. The number of those in training started rising in 1974 and the attendances at Selection Conferences began to rise significantly from 1975-76. We may note that the 1984 Establishment figure for Stipendiary Deaconesses and Lay Workers agreed by the House of Bishops was 422, though at the end of 1983 there were 425 actually in post (these do not include the Church Army).

76. So far as educational qualifications of recommended candidates are concerned, tabulated details only exist for 1981-1983. It would appear that 55-60 per cent have still been educated at Grammar Schools and that rather more than half have a degree, or equivalent qualification. Of those with professional qualifications about 70 per cent are College of Education trained teachers; consistently the next group are nurses but they only represent some 10-15 per cent.

77. In order to probe deeper behind these figures, a number of Diocesan Lay Ministry Advisers (DLMAs) were asked whether they had had a rise in the

24

number of women coming forward for selection in their dioceses in the last ten years and if they had any comments on the calibre of the candidates. Almost all reported a rise, some slow, some considerable. Of one large diocese, the DLMA reports: 'Between 1974 and 1979 inclusive, the number of Recommended Candidates has averaged out at six. From 1980 to 1983 the average per year has been twelve. If I had gone back to the period 1970 to 1973, the average would have been about three a year.'

78. Another DLMA, reporting, 'a considerable increase', adds: 'In fact so many are offering that the Bishop. . . has been getting a bit nervous about their eventual employment.' It was precisely this anxiety, that when women came out of training there might be no employment for them, which led to the appointment of a woman with wide experience of ministry to a part time post at Lambeth to make sure that all new entrants were placed (a comparable task to that performed at Lambeth in overseeing the allocation of Deacons.) A number of DLMAs comment on the high calibre of the candidates, both academically and otherwise. Several refer to their maturity. One DLMA comments: 'Spiritually very mature'. Another says: 'Our recent candidates have included two barristers, a head mistress of a school for the handicapped, a careers officer, a senior personnel officer, a distinguished author.' Another comments: 'Applicants in this year have come strictly in two categories, namely mainly married women for NSM Deaconess, who I think are of average to good calibre, and four girls who are single, comparatively young, and in calibre far above the average young man'. This DLMA is also Diocesan Director of Ordinands.

79. The DLMAs were also asked: 'Why, in your opinion, at a time when the number of men coming forward for ordination has declined (or remained at a low figure), have women been coming forward for ministry in increasing numbers?' Most do not profess to know the answer, but a number think that all the discussion about women's ministry has led to an understanding that there is a role for them in the Church. Some explicitly mention the discussions on the ordination of women or the hope of women that during their ministry it will become possible to be ordained priest. Others mention new possibilities of training for NSM and training locally. Another mentions joint training, another the effect of good women Readers, another greater opportunities in the parishes of real tasks. One DLMA (who is also a selector) writes: 'I suspect that the greater proportion of women going into ministry find their vocation through suffering — divorce, sickness, bereavement, spinsterhood. . . their suffering seems to be a female vocation.'

A very marked increase in deaconess ordinations

80. In 1969, there were 81 deaconesses and 282 lay workers working full

time. In 1979, the deaconesses outnumbered the licensed lay workers, and in December 1983, the figures were 312 deaconesses and 113 lay workers. (These figures do not include CA Sisters, a total of 59 were in various forms of work). The reasons for this change seem fairly clear: since 1977 candidates have been able to offer for deaconess ordination at the time of their selection for training, whereas previously a woman had to serve for two years as a licensed lay worker before a further selection for deaconess ordination. Since that time an increasing number have done just that and the number of candidates for the ministry of licensed lay worker has dwindled to a trickle. At the same time, a considerable number of those who were already serving as licensed lay workers asked to be considered for ordination. It may be that, ambiguous though the status of the deaconess has been, it has been clearer, at least in the eyes of the secular world, than that of a licensed lay worker. It may be that the legislation to enable women to become deacons has accelerated this move.

Some increase in posts of responsibility for women

81. The DLMAs were asked whether in their diocese they had women working in jobs of greater responsibility and of what sort they were. In particular, were any women in pastoral charge and had these jobs increased? It may be useful to summarise the answers under two headings: those in pastoral charge and those in other posts.

In pastoral charge

There are a number of cases where women are acting as Team Vicars or are in charge of an area of a parish, or a daughter church. There are also some places where a woman is in pastoral charge of a parish. Several of these posts seem to be in ecumenical settings. Some dioceses say they are working on this possibility: others do not see it as likely in their situation. One DLMA sounds a note of warning:

> The experience in this Diocese of attempting to give added responsibility within the parish structure is not a happy one. It always happens that such a post is proposed because of certain difficulties. The woman then goes in and inherits the legacy of a good deal of past bitterness as a result of negotiations between the parish and 'them' at diocesan headquarters. This has little to do with the woman herself, and much more to do with the fact that they feel they have been unfairly deprived of their own vicar.

Other Posts

82. There are a number of women in various diocesan education posts, University and Polytechnic and Hospital Chaplains, a Diocesan Missioner, and on the staff of a theological college. In a number of Dioceses the DDO is also the DLMA but Worcester Diocese has recently appointed a deaconess to be both DDO and DLMA.

A further point needs to be made. The increase of married women offering for ministry poses problems for some dioceses. If they are offering for NSM the diocese may feel able to send them forward for selection. But one diocese, where money is a problem, has decided that it cannot accept a married woman for *stipendiary* ministry if she is not able to be mobile, lest it prevent the acceptance of someone who is freely deployable. They have a similar policy concerning NSM priests who wish to go stipendiary: they must be mobile.

What Sort of Ministry?

83. The stories of women in ministry are beginning to be told, e.g. Margaret Cundiff, *Called to be me.* and *Follow On* (Triangle, 1982 and 1983). It may be that following the example of the Episcopal Church USA we should set up an Oral History Project to record on tape, before it is too late, the experience of women in ministry, especially some of the older pioneers.

84. Many women in ministry, probably most, are exercising a traditional style of ministry and appear to be happy to do so, unless and until 'the shoe pinches' at some point and their ministry and ability to serve is diminished. But does this mean that all difficulties would be resolved by ordination?

85. It is here that the experience of women priests in other parts of the Anglican Communion is important: many of them have been quite happy to fit into existing patterns and to find in them a fulfilling ministry. Others are raising questions: some of these questions are similar to those raised in the ACCM paper *Women in Training* (see below and Appendix IV): others are fundamentally questioning not orders of ministry but rather the ordering of ministry and current practice. It may be that the life experience of women leads them to question pyramidical structures of ministry and to look for more co-operative ones: is the image of a circle rather than of a pyramid closer to the Gospel pattern of corporate ministry? And would it be better not only for the people of the parish but also for the ministry itself?

86. Reflection on this area inevitably brings in the Tiller Report (*A Strategy for the Church's Ministry*, John Tiller CIO, 1983). One short section deals with the ordination of women.

(3) The Ordination of Women
While I personally expect with some confidence that women will be admitted to the Order of Priests during the period covered by this report there is but one major respect in which the strategy could be affected by the timing of the Church's decision on this matter. If women were to be ordained as priests in the very near future then the traditional policy of GS 374 would once again become a realistic option. This is the one way in which the numbers of stipendiary clergy could be rapidly increased: there are existing women ministers (333 stipendiaries in 1982)

who in most cases have been fully trained to the requirements for ordinands, and in many cases are conscious of a call to ordination as priests. The number of women candidates has greatly increased in recent years, and there is good hope that future combined numbers of men and women offering for stipendiary ministry would be well up to the target range of 400/450 recommendations each year. Moreover, the cost to the Church of training and maintaining such numbers in the stipendiary ministry would be little affected, because the stipendiary women ministers *already exist:* it is simply a question of whether they are to be priests or not. I do not believe that this issue is best determined by considering the factor of the shortage of stipendiary clergy alone, and even if a decision on this matter had already been taken, the strategy set out in this report would still be offered as a better way for the future. Under those circumstances, however, it would also be possible for the Church to continue depending on the familiar strengths of its full-time parochial ministry. There are many ways in which the style of ministry is affected by the sex of the minister; and the Church is surely impoverished by its failure to make full use of the potential ministry of women: nevertheless the broad strategy here advocated is one which can be pursued whatever the proportions of men and women engaged in each category of ministry. (p.50)

87. More important perhaps is the whole thrust of the Report, with its radical desire to return to a shared ministry rooted in the local community. (If any woman were to seek ordination in order to 'make it' into a male power structure she will find the Tiller Report as disturbing and threatening as some clergy have.) The Church of England, partly because of the shortage of men candidates for Stipendiary ministry, is having to ask some of the real questions on ministry.

A relatively recent phenomenon, but an increasingly important one, is that of 'Joint Ministries', a partnership in ministry between husband and wife who are, for example, priest and deaconess. The report of a recent consultation on such ministries says:

> It is not possile to foresee completely where the growing number of women in ministry and an increasing number of couples in ministry will lead us. We have to try to make sense of a developing situation. Furthermore, so long as the Church of England has the ordination of women to the priesthood on its agenda, while unresolved in practice, any statement about joint-ministries will be descriptive of an interim situation. (*Joint Ministries Consultation,* ACCM Occasional Paper No.16, 1984)

Perhaps the real need is to bring the thinking on shared ministry, Non-Stipendiary ministry, Local ministry, Ordained and Lay, closer together with the debate on the ordination of women to priesthood.

88. Something needs to be said about training for this ministry. *Women in Training* (ACCM Occasional Paper No.14, 1983) contains some reflections by a group of women staff members of Theological Colleges and Courses. Much of this valuable paper is reproduced as Appendix IV. Here we quote from part of the Introduction.

28

Introduction: A Changing Situation

1. The last twenty years have seen enormous changes in the contribution women make to professional ministry in all English churches and the Church of England is no exception. In spite of the official position in regard to the ordination of women to the priesthood, there are many more opportunities for women both in parochial and specialist ministries. Changes have been made also in the selection and training of women for the Order of Deaconess and for Accredited Lay Ministry. Women attend selection centres alongside men seeking ordination to the priesthood and are trained in the same way in mixed theological colleges. Since the closure of the women's training houses almost all colleges have opened their doors to women. Inevitably with the smaller numbers of women, they are very much in the minority in the colleges but nevertheless increasingly make a significant contribution to the worship, life and work of the communities, helping to demonstrate that professional ministry must be a partnership involving women and men. Most colleges also have one or more women on their staff teaching a variety of courses. The women staff are not specifically responsible for the women students. There has been a clear recognition of the importance of having a mixed staff to provide complementary patterns of ministry for those in training.

2. All of these changes are to be welcomed. Strangely, however, little thought seems to have been given to the content and style of the training given to the women. They receive exactly the same training as the men to be ordained to the priesthood in spite of the fact that the Church has no intention of ordaining them as priests. More and more women are beginning to question both the content of the courses as well as the style and methods of training. They are asking whether the assumption that no changes were necessary when women were brought into the colleges was in fact a correct one.

3. There is now sufficient experience of women in theological colleges to begin to investigate whether we have too readily drafted women into male structures and prepared them for ministry using only male role models. (pp.5-6)

89. We must now turn to the question of those women who believe they experience a call to priesthood. Something has been said on this in GS 104 (pp.77-78) and in GS Misc 88, (p.42, para.146). There is no doubt that the church-wide debate from 1972-1975 and the return of the issue in 1978 raised many hopes: inevitably a deep sense of disappointment and frustration followed.

90. The stories of some of these women who feel they are waiting are now appearing in print. Reference has already been made to Margaret Cundiff's two books: other stories are to be found in Mary Tanner's chapter 'Called to Priesthood: Interpreting Women's Experience' in *Feminine in the Church* (SPCK, 1984).

91. Nevertheless, there exists a quite proper anxiety that concentration on the ordination of women as deacons and efforts to secure the opening of the

priesthood for women, might have the effect of submerging the proper quest for a truly lay involvement in ministry. One DLMA, in reply to the questions referred to in a previous section, pleaded for proper consideration of the whole area of training accredited lay people. Who is to train those lay people whose centre is *in* the world, and on whom the major responsibility for today's mission must lie, is a question urgently raised by Ruth Etchells of St John's College, Durham. The relevance of all this to our concern must surely be the hope that, if women were to become priests, they would not allow themselves to be imprisoned in a priestly caste nor be cut off from other women in the church.

92. At the time of the 1978 debate, and subsequently, there were voices raised among the opponents of the ordination of women, asking for a real ministry of women. The Bishop of London seems to have hopes of this through the diaconate. But these hopes still await any very clear articulation. Might not part of the current debate be usefully given to working out together what this could mean for the church and for those women who are called to ministry? Sadly, such a call for a real women's ministry, when translated into practical terms, often turns out to be no more than women *already* do in the Church of England today.

93. It is well to realise that, in contrast to many other Churches, (e.g. the Lutheran Church of Sweden or some other Anglican Provinces) the Church of England allows to lay persons a considerable share in the conduct of worship. Thus the experience of women leading in worship, whether deaconesses, licensed lay workers or Readers, has changed the expectations of many people. It should be noted that the number of women Readers listed in the Church Statistics rose from nine in 1969 to 856 in 1982, about 12 per cent of the total, but that, in the same year, the 463 women in Reader training represented some 27 per cent.

IV DEVELOPMENTS WITHIN THE ANGLICAN COMMUNION

General

94. The Anglican Consultative Council, meeting in Ontario in 1979, considered both the inter-Anglican and the ecumenical aspects of the Ordination of Women (for the latter, see Chapter V)

> 5 Inter-Anglican Dialogue on Women in the Priesthood
> In his review at the beginning of ACC4, the Secretary General said:
>> 'It is now clearly recognised that the Anglican Communion contains women priests, that in the present situation some member Churches ordain women and some do not, and no Church is requiring another to change. What any particular Church may decide does not alter this.'
>
> The careful discussion of the subject of women in the priesthood by the Lambeth Conference of 1978 is known and its advice has found general acceptance. In its Resolution (LCR 21.5c(i)) it requested the ACC 'to use its good offices to promote dialogue between those member Churches which ordain women and those which do not, with a view to exploring ways in which the fullest use can be made of women's gifts within the total ministry of the Church in our Communion'.
>
> The Council desires to promote such dialogue, recognising that the member Churches fall generally into four categories:
> (1) those which have acted to ordain women to the priesthood
> (2) those which have rejected such action
> (3) those which have agreed there are no fundamental theological objections to such ordinations but have not yet acted to make it possible
> (4) those for which the issue is still to be resolved.
>
> Within each of these categories there are those individuals who hold different views, and yet are loyal Anglicans.
>
> Because of these different positions and because we live in a mobile society, continuing dialogue is essential to help us understand all the issues involved, and also to develop guidelines for action which will respect the integrity of both persons and provinces. It is important to recognise that the dialogue required is not one or two international meetings but a wide variety of many types of meetings involving different groups of people dealing with particular areas of concern. Among the theological issues, there is an urgent need to study how member Churches can remain in communion with one another when there is no longer full acceptance and mutuality of ordained ministry. Practical issues here include the use of conscience clauses and the mobility of women priests. (See LC Report, 1978, p.81)
>
> In order that it may be creative rather than destructive, the Council suggests that the goals of dialogue should be:
> 1. to enable all to come to a deeper understanding of the truth of God's will for His Church;

2.	to encourage and strengthen the bonds of fellowship and unity within the Anglican Communion.

Resolution 15: Inter-Anglican Dialogue on Women in the Priesthood
The Council:

1.	Affirms the need of dialogue between member Churches which take different positions concerning the principle of the Ordination of Women to the Priesthood, and about the practical and theological issues which arise from the fact that some Provinces ordain women to the Priesthood and others do not.

2.	urges the member Churches, when possible, to take an active part in studying together the community of men and women in the Church, and ways in which the fullest use can be made of the gifts of both men and women within the total ministry.

3.	requests the Secretary General to facilitate such dialogue, bearing in mind the above recommendations.

4.	urges the Primates when they meet in November to develop guidelines for Provinces regarding sending or receiving of women priests either for visits or on the occasion of a change of residence. (*ACC4 Report*, 1979, pp.45, 46)

95. In the Report of the Section on Unity, consideration is given to the 'Ecumenical Consequences of the Ordination of Women'. In Resolution 8 which follows, the ACC 'affirms the importance of ecumenical participation in inter-Anglican dialogue'on this matter, (see Chapter V for text of Report and Resolution).

96. In November 1979, the Primates' Meeting approved Guidelines concerning Women Priests who visit other Provinces.

(1) Quotes Resolution 15, para: 4 of ACC 4 (see above)

(2) 'In considering this matter, the Primates had in mind Paragraph 6 of Resolution 21 of the 1978 Lambeth Conference Report': (see GS Misc. 88, page 8)

(3) The Primates wish to acknowledge the grateful appreciation of the whole Anglican Communion for the rich and generous ministry, within the renewed understanding of the total ministry of the Church, exercised by women in our Church in every part of the world, and to express the hope that every encouragement will be given to the development of such ministries as may be appropriate in each Province.

(4) Meanwhile in response to the ACC Resolution quoted above the Primates recommend:

(a)	that the customary procedures and courtesies regarding the exercise of ministry in other Provinces be followed, namely

(b)	that women priests who have been canonically ordained in their own Province and who subsequently move, either for long or short periods to another Province, should abide by the relevant formal resolutions or regulations of that Province.

	No-one, ordained or lay, male or female, has any inherent right to exercise a duly authorised ministry in any diocese. Permission to exercise a ministry rests with the bishop of the Diocese.

(c)   That where a Province has made no formal decision regarding women priests the direction of the diocesan bishop, made after consultation with the Primate of the Province, should be followed.

(5) Finally, the Primates wish to re-affirm what was said by ACC 4 in Resolution 15 paras. 1-3 (see above) (GS Misc. 127)

97. ACC5 met at Newcastle-upon-Tyne in 1981. In the Section 'Growing in our Ministries' is a series of Questions for the Anglican Communion, and among them:

3. How does the church live with different developments in the pattern of ordained ministry that may seem unwise to some, but proper and wise to others?
5. How do Provinces and dioceses that have ordained women and those who have not, listen to and remain open to one another?

The Section adds:

We do not see clear answers to any of these questions. Indeed many of us are passionately at one or the other extreme of many of them. But we believe it to be a special vocation of the Anglican Communion, which embodies all these differences, to stay with the pain, to grow through it into the ministry to which we are called.
(*ACC 5 Report 1981*, pp.50, 51)

98. In their Report on ACC 5, the Church of England members of the ACC had this to say:

Although not a matter for formal debate at Newcastle the growing number of women priests, and the increasing frustration of many Anglicans (particularly bishops) in Canada, New Zealand and the U.S.A. at England's refusal to allow their priestly ministry on visits here, together constitute a bigger stress on the unity of the Communion than may be generally recognised in this country.
(GS Misc 152, para. 13)

99. ACC6, meeting in Nigeria in 1984, in the section on Ecumenical Concerns, considered the question of Full Communion.

While not wishing to offer a complete and final definition of *full communion* the term surely implies *at least* that the ministry of one Church or Province is in fact accepted by another, except in individual cases on individual and personal grounds — thus excluding the unacceptability of whole categories within the ministry of a particular Church. This applies both to the few remaining non-episcopally ordained presbyters of the Church of South India and to women ordained to the priesthood in the Anglican Communion when visiting Provinces which do not so ordain.

As far as the ordination of women is concerned it appears that no action has been taken on Resolutions 8 and 15 of ACC-4 which proposed inter-Anglican dialogue on Women in the Priesthood with ecumenical participation from those Churches with which the Communion is in dialogue. These resolutions were in accord with decisions of the Lambeth Conference of 1978, Resolution 21, particularly paragraphs 5, 6 and 7.

Full Communion normally implies full acceptability of ordained ministries, but as the number of women priests increases, the non-acceptability of their ministry in some Provinces is being seen as calling into question the integrity of the ministry and episcopate in those Provinces which ordain women. The provisions of Lambeth 1978, Resolution 21: 6(a) and (b) regarding mutual respect for each other's convictions requires more than a blanket refusal to allow women ordained in other Provinces to officiate under any circumstances on the one hand, and on the other hand less than an assertion of rights to exercise such ministry under any and all circumstances.

What seems a reasonable approach is for Provinces not ordaining women to allow ordained women from abroad to exercise their ministry on particular occasions during temporary visits, but not to go further without due synodical approval. We consider this approach would carry out the advice of Lambeth 1978 (referred to above) to respect each other's convictions and assist in maintaining full communion between Provinces of the Communion.

100. Commenting on this section of the Report, Patricia Bays of Canada, who chaired this section, noted that in drafting the resolution the section had been 'sensitive to hurts on both sides', and recognised that in some cultures the sacramental ministry of women would not be considered appropriate. Therefore, she said, the resolution was not intended to demand that every Province extend such hospitality at this time, but rather to urge consideration of the matter in light of the fact that Full Communion is impaired by one Province's failure to recognise the duly ordained priests of another.

The Present Position within Churches/Provinces

101. For completeness sake, all Churches/Provinces are listed for which information is available. Where such information is to be found in GS 104 and/or GS Misc. 88 the reference is indicated and only in those cases where there have been developments since 1978 is new material added. (Note on statistics: these have been obtained from ACC, supplemented from other sources. They must be regarded as approximate figures since Churches do not usually maintain separate lists of women clergy and are sometimes dependent on a Pension Fund list or information from a deployment list.)

CHURCHES WHICH ORDAIN WOMEN AS PRIESTS AND DEACONS
Canada (GS Misc 88. para.31)
102. In summer 1984 there were approximately 127 women clergy, (97 priests and 30 deacons). This figure is based on information from an unofficial source but is probably fairly accurate: it includes at least two retired priests. These 127 women clergy are currently spread over 20 dioceses from all four Provinces. Ten dioceses do not have women clergy: Western Newfoundland, Fredericton, Ontario, Keewatin, Saskatchewan, Saskatoon,

Calgary, British Columbia, the Arctic and Moosonee, (the latter diocese has, however, previously had women clergy). In only one diocese, Kootenay, does it seem that the bishop, while ordaining women to the diaconate, does not intend to ordain women as priests. It is thought that, while in some dioceses refusal to ordain women may be due to objection in principle, in others it may be because there is a shortage of suitable jobs for them. The dioceses with the largest number of women clergy are Toronto (23) and Niagara (14). Of the 127 women clergy, at least 16 were in charge of a parish by 1982-83. Women serve in rural as well as urban areas and some are in parishes of 3, 4, 5 and even 14 points (communities). In this respect, it is well to recall that, in the Anglican Church of Canada, a number of women, including deaconesses, have in the past served in remote areas, sometimes in charge of some isolated church and community. Some of these women are now priests in the Canadian Church and it would seem that this experience helped the Anglican Church of Canada in its acceptance of the ministry of women priests. Nevertheless some difficulties have been experienced, particularly perhaps among younger women, especially in rural areas. Here an older, more mature woman, may find greater acceptance (especially if she clearly enjoys rural ministry and meets conservative expectations).

103. In 1980, the General Synod of the Anglican Church of Canada passed two Acts:

Act 21. That this Synod commend to the dioceses that they develop and implement policies and strategies for the fuller participation of women in the leadership and councils of the Church.

Act 22. That this Synod encourage affirmative action to ensure more rapid progress toward sexual equality of opportunity in filling senior positions at the national and diocesan levels of the Church.

104. In November 1981, Archbishop Scott asked women priests to meet with him at Winnipeg, because, in 1975, he had promised to evaluate the work of ordained women five years after the first ordination. 90 per cent of the women priests came and, as experiences were shared, it became evident that women felt that their orders were being compromised by the operation of the Conscience Clause (enacted at the time of the acceptance of the ordination of women). When Archbishop Scott brought detailed examples of this to the attention of the National Executive Council and the House of Bishops, they initiated a re-opening of the Conscience Clause. The National Executive Council forwarded to the 1983 General Synod for its approval a statement on 'the pastoral interpretation of the continuing use of the Conscience Clause by those who remain unable to accept the ordination of women to the priesthood.' This included:

We recognise and affirm the continuing validity of the Conscience Clause for those who belonged to the Anglican Church of Canada at the time it was passed.

While continuing to recognise the rights of individual consciences, we believe that those who now come to membership or to any office or ministry in our Church must recognise and accept that the ministry of women priests must also be protected conscientiously as the expressed will of our Church.

105. The House of Bishops, meeting before the General Synod, prepared their own resolution, so that of the Executive Council was not pursued and the Bishops' resolution passed with an overwhelming majority. It reads:

Resolution 92.
1. That this General Synod concur with the following statement of the House of Bishops concerning the Conscience Clause, June 1983.
2. The Archbishops and Bishops of the Anglican Church of Canada are agreed that through the General Synod of 1975 the Anglican Church of Canada has expressed its will that women may be ordained to the Priesthood.
3. It is also agreed that the Conscience Clause which was approved at the time of this change in policy should continue in force. The House, however, deplores the misapplication which some members of the Church have made of the Clause.
4. No action which questions the integrity of any priest or postulant on grounds of sex alone can be defended by an appeal to the Clause.
5. The House honours women priests, upholds them in its prayers, and desires only that God's will may be done in and through all priests whether female or male.
6. Christian love cannot be legislated, but needs to be practised and demonstrated more effectively in order to realize the community which belongs in the Body of Christ.

106. The General Synod of 1983 re-affirmed Acts 21 and 22 of the 1980 General Synod and also passed Resolution 60:

Be it resolved that: in this Church now all functions, offices and ministries, in the jurisdiction of General Synod, be open equally to men and women.

Hong Kong (GS 104, paras. 227-233 and GS Misc 88, para.32)

107. The number of women priests serving in the Diocese of Hong Kong in 1983 is given as four (with a note that one would retire in August 1983): two in charge of parishes and two school staff. There is also a married woman priest from the U.S.A., serving as an assistant in a parish. The Rev Li Tim Oi is not serving in the Diocese but in the Anglican Church of Canada, where she is listed among the Toronto clergy.

Kenya (GS Misc 88, para.48)

108. In 1976 the House of Bishops accepted 'in principle' and in 1978 the Provincial Standing Committee voted to give the go ahead to the ordination of women as priests and deacons. On this basis, Dr Henry Okullu, Bishop of Maseno South, ordained Mrs Lucia Okuthe as a deacon after she had been

approved by the Diocesan Synod. But in November 1982 the Provincial Synod declared that the 1978 action of the Standing Committee was unprocedural. It passed a motion reaffirming that women might be ordained both as deacons and priests but added that, while this principle was 'commendable', dioceses should nevertheless discuss the issue fully and report back to the Provincial Synod for a final decision to be made. Hence, the resolution concludes, 'there shall be no ordination of women in any diocese within the province in any circumstances whatsoever until this Synod's said final decision at its next meeting.'

109. Bishop Okullu, acting with the support of his diocese, proceeded nevertheless to ordain Mrs Okuthe as priest on 2 January 1983. She was subsequently appointed Vicar of the new parish of Muhoroni.

New Zealand (GS 104, para. 235; and GS Misc 88, paras. 33-34)

110. In 1984, there were about 55 women clergy, of which perhaps a quarter are deacons. Twenty-three of these are in the diocese of Auckland, but only one diocese has none. New Zealand has no Conscience Clause and it is understood that, when the present Bishop of Nelson retires, the New Zealand Church will have no more bishops who are not willing to ordain women. Ten women are Vicars or Priests-in-charge and four are in College or School Chaplaincy work. There are a few permanent deacons (by their own choice).

111. It is reported that there appears to be some resistance to making appointments of women priests to positions of sole pastoral responsibility in parishes. While it is recognised that there is a time lag between adopting a policy of ordaining women as priests and the attainment of full equality of deployment, it would appear that this reluctance stems also from other factors (personality, marital status etc). It would also seem that lay attitudes have been slower to change than those of the clergy. (An analysis of clergy attitudes in 1983 indicated that only 14.4 per cent had hesitations about the decision to ordain women.) One woman priest comments on the definite decline in numbers as one moves south, due partly to a much smaller population in the South Island but also reflecting a more conservative attitude.

112. One significant point is that more than half the women clergy in New Zealand are non-stipendiary. It has been said that the availability of the non-stipendiary style of ordained ministry allows a woman to combine an ordained ministry with family and community responsibilities. But does it also reflect a desire to exercise priestly ministry while not embracing the clerical profession? If most of these non-stipendiaries are married women supported by their husbands, does this raise some questions of principle?

113. The emergence of the 'clergy couple' is also noted: women who are motivated towards ordination are beginning to opt for theological study while their husbands are in training for priesthood.

Uganda

114. In 1977 a number of women were ordained deacon. It was envisaged that they would be ordained priest in due course but, after the 1978 Lambeth Conference, no further action was taken. There are now 27 women deacons. However, in December 1983, Bishop Festo Kivengere (Kigezi) ordained three women priests. It appears that this move was irregular but a subsequent meeting of the House of Bishops and Provincial Assembly voted that there were no objections in principle and left the matter to each Bishop to act as he felt fit.

United States of America (GS 104 para.239; GS Misc 88, paras.35-38)

115. *The statistical information* is available (from various sources) in considerable detail. In April 1984, there were 744 women clergy (474 priests and 270 deacons). For 108 of these (52 priests and 56 deacons) information concerning their work is not known. Information for the remaining 636 may be summarised as follows:

Rector/Vicar	81
Interim Vicar/In charge	24 (including 2 deacons in charge)
Co-Pastor	7 (1 deacon)
Assistant/Associate	288 (117 deacons)
Canon of Cathedral	6
College/School Chaplain	36 (6 deacons)
Hospital/Prison Chaplain	29 (12 deacons)
Teachers in College/Seminary	19 (2 deacons)
Church related Administrative or Special Positions	42 (16 deacons)
Religious Orders	8 (4 priests, 4 deacons)
Non-Stipendiary	52 (29 priests, 23 deacons)
At home	6 (4 priests, 2 deacons)
Retired	28 (3 priests, 25 deacons)
Unemployed	10 (6 priests, 4 deacons)

The significant number of women deacons holding responsible posts may be due in part to the existence of a number of men and women permanent deacons and to the existence of dioceses which will ordain women as deacons but not as priests.

116. *The distribution of women clergy* in the Episcopal Church in the USA (ECUSA), is very uneven. First of all, of the 115 dioceses, 40 per cent

appear to have no women priest *canonically* resident: in some of these, women may be *physically* resident but in such dioceses they are unlikely to function as clergy; in some of these dioceses women are ordained as deacons, but not as priests. However, 18 of these are missionary dioceses (mainly in Central and South America, the Caribbean and the Philippines). The 27 dioceses in mainland U.S.A. which have no canonically resident clergy are: Albany, Central Florida, Easton, Eau Claire, Fond du Lac, Florida, Georgia, Lousiana, Lexington, Long Island, Milwaukee, Nebraska, Northern Indiana, North Western Pennsylvania (previously Erie), Northwest Texas, Oklahoma, Quincy, San Diego, San Joaquin, South Carolina, South Dakota, Springfield, Southern Virginia, Southwest Florida, Western Kansas, Western Louisiana and West Missouri.

117. Where a diocese has no women priests this may be because the bishop will not ordain women or it may be that the Diocesan Standing Committee will not accept them. Some bishops allow their Suffragans to ordain women. Few dioceses have as many as ten women clergy: the thirteen dioceses in which a significant number of women clergy are canonically or physically resident are: New York, Michigan, Massachusetts, California, Virginia, Connecticut, Pennslvania, Chicago, New Jersey, Minnesota, Newark, Rio Grande and Washington. From this list it will be seen that women clergy are somewhat concentrated in the Eastern States, California and Pacific States, and parts of the Mid-West.

118. *The Employment Situation* for women is not easy. It will be seen that of the 376 women priests known to be in stipendiary ministry, no less than 171 are Assistants or Associates (45 per cent). While a number of these may be in the first years of their ministry or may prefer for personal reasons (e.g. family) to remain as Assistants, there is some evidence that women find it harder than men to move into more senior posts. In 1982, there were no women Rectors in the diocese of Massachussets and only one in New York City. In 1982 the Dean of General Theological Seminary commented that the men who were the seminary contemporaries of the first women priests would at that time expect to become Rectors and if the vestries did not call women then something was wrong. (Could it be that the Episcopal Church, while legislating to ordain women as priests did little to change the fixed expectations of the lay members of vestries as they set about calling a new Rector?) It must however be recalled that, in certain areas at least, the Episcopal Church already has more men clergy than it can easily employ: in 1982, there were said to be 200 clergy who earned their living otherwise than from stipendiary ministry in the diocese of New York. It would seem that a number of women either work (or are paid) part time for stipendiary ministry. The next few years will show whether this is a passing phase or a continuing pattern.

119. *Enrolment of Women* in seven of the ten accredited seminaries of the Episcopal Church shows that there are 214 women out of 606 students (35 per cent). In the Episcopal Divinity School, Cambridge, Mass. women students are 63 per cent and at Church Divinity School of the Pacific, Berkeley, California they are 48 per cent. Women are on the staff of seminaries.

CHURCHES WHICH HAVE APPROVED THE ORDINATION OF WOMEN TO THE PRIESTHOOD WITHOUT SUBSEQUENT ACTION

Brazil (GS Misc 88, para. 61)

120. The recent meeting of the Provincial Synod of the Anglican Church of Brazil — the Igreja Episcopal do Brasil — has voted overwhelmingly in favour of the ordination of women.
The voting was as follows:

	For	*Against*
Bishops	5	0
Clergy	12	1
Laity	12	1

Burma (GS104, para. 234)

121. No further information.

The Indian Ocean (GS Misc 88, para.41)

122. No further information.

Ireland (GS Misc 88, paras. 42-46)

123. After the General Synod resolution of May 1976, the dioceses voted on the matter in their Synods. In 1980, a motion that leave be granted for a bill to be introduced in the 1981 session for the ordination of women failed to achieve the needed two-thirds majority. In May 1984 the General Synod approved in principle the ordination of women as deacons and proceeded to the enabling legislation.

Japan (GS Misc 88, para. 47)

124. No further information.

Wales (GS 104, para. 237; GS Misc 88, paras. 49-51)

125. The Governing Body of the Church in Wales agreed to have women deacons in 1980. This allowed for the ordination of present deaconesses to the Order of Deacon. The first ordinations took place in 1980. In 1983 there were 15 deacons: 8 parochial staff, 1 assistant hospital chaplain and 5 non-stipendiary (one of these on a college staff).

CHURCHES WHICH HAVE APPROVED THE ORDINATION OF WOMEN TO THE PRIESTHOOD WHERE ACTION IS PENDING

Australia

126. The General Synod of the Church voted in 1977 that there were no theological objections constituting a barrier to the ordination to the diaconate, priesthood and the episcopate. The move put in action a process of legislation which, because the General Synod meets only every four years, would probably take 12-20 years. 1981 General Synod approved draft legislation which is now before the dioceses. This seems likely to be defeated. According to the constitution of the Church, as well as having the support of three-quarters of all dioceses, it must also have the support of all metropolitan dioceses. Already the Metropolitan Diocese of Adelaide is reported to have voted 'no'.

PROVINCES WHICH HAVE EITHER REJECTED OR POSTPONED POSITIVE ACTION

Central Africa (GS 104. para. 240 and GS Misc 88, para. 55)

127. No further information.

Diocese of Singapore (GS Misc 88, para.57)

128. No further information.

Sri Lanka (GS Misc 88, para. 56)

129. Will not ordain women for cultural reasons.

The South Pacific Anglican Council (GS 104, para. 236 and GS Misc 88, para. 58)

130. The Bishops who are members of this Council represent the Provinces of Papua New Guinea, Melanesia and the diocese of Polynesia which is a missionary diocese of the Church of New Zealand. Melanesia and Papua New Guinea report that they will never ordain their own women for cultural reasons but are going to consider whether or not to accept the ministrations of women ordained in New Zealand.

Tanzania (GS Misc 88, para. 59)

131. No further information.

West Africa (GS Misc 88, para. 66)

132. The situation here is unclear: while it was still part of the Episcopal Church USA, the diocese of Liberia received a woman priest from the United States. In 1982, Liberia joined the Province of West Africa. (The 1984 figure for ECUSA still lists Liberia but with no women clergy.) The Province has now decided not to accept visiting women clergy.

West Indies (GS Misc 88, para.54)

133. No further information.

CHURCHES WHICH HAVE APPROVED WOMEN DEACONS IN PRINCIPLE AND WHERE ACTION IS PENDING

South Africa (GS Misc 88, para. 53)

134. In December 1982 the General Synod agreed to the Ordination of Women to the Diaconate and asked the House of Bishops to select and train suitable candidates.

CHURCHES WHICH HAVE VOTED AGAINST WOMEN DEACONS

Scottish Episcopal Church (GS 104, para. 238; GS Misc 88, para. 52)

135. The November 1981 meeting of the Church's General Synod failed to achieve two-thirds support in its First Chamber, although it was carried overwhelmingly in its Second Chamber. The matter therefore lapsed.

CHURCHES FROM WHICH NO ACTION HAS AS YET BEEN REPORTED

136. *Burundi, Rwanda and Zaire*
Jerusalem and the Middle East
Nigeria
Anglican Council of South America
The Sudan

V THE ECUMENICAL EVIDENCE

General

137. *The Anglican Consultative Council* at its 1979 meeting in Canada (ACC4), in its Section Report on Unity had this to say:

12 Ecumenical Consequences of the Ordination of Women

In ecumenical relations the ordination of women creates at least three problems:

1   caused by member Churches which ordain women, for those non-Anglican Churches which do not;

2   caused by member Churches which have decided not to ordain women, for those non-Anglican Churches which do;

3   caused by resulting Anglican sacramental disunity, for those non-Anglican Churches with which Anglicans are seeking full communion.

(1) The Dialogue with Churches which are opposed in principle to the ordination of women has already begun, in the Athens meeting of the Anglican-Orthodox Joint Doctrinal Discussions, and in the Anglican-Roman Catholic Versailles Consultation: there has also been discussion between the Church of England and the Old Catholic Churches. We hope that the Anglican Orthodox Joint Doctrinal Discussions will continue to consider the question and that it will arise in the dialogue with the Roman Catholic Church in the Joint Commission which we hope will follow the present ARCIC.

(2) The decision of the Church of England not to proceed to the ordination of women is likely to cause problems for ecumenical negotiations in England in the Churches' Council for Covenanting, especially on the question of the recognition or non-recognition of women ministers in the non-Anglican Churches. The same problem is likely to arise elsewhere.

(3)Within our Communion some Anglicans are unable in conscience to recognise the ministry of canonically ordained women priests. Likewise some Provinces and even dioceses within Provinces do not authorize women priests who are in good standing in their home Province, to exercise a sacramental ministry. These facts seriously call in question the reality of that acceptance of each other's members and ministry which 'being in communion with' has up to now implied. They also constitute an anomalous situation which detracts from the proper universality of the ministerial priesthood. Though these are principally problems for the Anglican Communion, they have ecumenical consequences; for at the heart of the present ecumenical quest lies the need for a mutually recognised ministry.

Resolution 8: Dialogue on Ordination of Women

Because of the ecumenical consequences of the ordination of women, the Council affirms the importance of ecumenical participation in inter-Anglican dialogue concerning this matter, particularly by those non-Anglican Churches with which Anglicans are already in national or international dialogue.(*ACC-4 Report*, pp.14-15)

(For ACC-4's specific commitments on relations with Roman Catholics and Orthodox, see below)

138. *The Faith and Order Commission* of the World Council of Churches, in the *Lima Text, Baptism, Eucharist and Ministry* (Faith and Order Paper No. 111, WCC, 1982) has this paragraph and commentary on the Ministry of Men and Women in the Church.

D The Ministry of Men and Women in the Church

18. Where Christ is present, human barriers are being broken. The Church is called to convey to the world the image of a new humanity. There is in Christ no male or female (Gal. 3:28). Both women and men must discover together their contributions to the service of Christ in the Church. The Church must discover the ministry which can be provided by women as well as that which can be provided by men. A deeper understanding of the comprehensiveness of ministry which reflects the interdependence of men and women needs to be more widely manifested in the life of the Church.

Though they agree on this need, the churches draw different conclusions as to the admission of women to the ordained ministry. An increasing number of churches have decided that there is no biblical or theological reason against ordaining women, and many of them have subsequently proceeded to do so. Yet many churches hold that the tradition of the Church in this regard must not be changed.

Commentary (18)

Those churches which practise the ordination of women do so because of their understanding of the Gospel and of the ministry. It rests for them on the deeply held theological conviction that the ordained ministry of the Church lacks fullness when it is limited to one sex. This theological conviction has been reinforced by their experience during the years in which they have included women in their ordained ministries. They have found that women's gifts are as wide and varied as men's and that their ministry is as fully blessed by the Holy Spirit as the ministry of men. None has found reason to reconsider its decision.

Those churches which do not practise the ordination of women consider that the force of nineteen centuries of tradition against the ordination of women must not be set aside. They believe that such a tradition cannot be dismissed as a lack of respect for the participation of women in the Church. They believe that there are theological issues concerning the nature of humanity and concerning Christology which lie at the heart of their convictions and understanding of the role of women in the Church.

The discussion of these practical and theological questions within the various churches and Christian traditions should be complemented by joint study and reflection within the ecumenical fellowship of all churches. (pp.23-24)

139. What might hardly be realised from this text, 'a cautious retreat from the much bolder Accra text' (i.e. text at Accra Faith and Order Commission meeting 1974), as Mary Tanner calls it, is that, throughout the latter part of the work on the Lima Text, the WCC had a study programme starting in 1977 and culminating in a conference in Sheffield in 1981, on 'The Community of Women and Men in the Church'. The concerns of this study were never fully reflected in the Lima Text.

140. Mary Tanner, a leading Anglican member of the Community Study and involved in the Faith and Order Commission, charts this lack of relationship between the two studies in an article: *Baptism, Eucharist and Ministry and the Community Study* (Midstream, July 1984). Of the Lima Text on Ministry she says:

> It sets out clearly the interdependence between the ministry of the whole people of God and the set apart ministry. There is no way here in which the ordained ministry can be understood either theologically or functionally as an order or a caste apart from the Christian community. 'All members of the believing community, ordained and lay, are interrelated'. It is in the eucharist where the representative nature of the ordained ministry is most clearly focussed. Here the ordained ministers are seen to focus 'the deep and all embracing communion between Christ and the members of his body'. Here, they also represent the presidency of Christ at the meal. In another passage the priesthood of the ordained ministry is further described as relating in two ways: 'ordained ministers are related, both to the priesthood of Christ, and to the priesthood of the Church'.

> It is at this point that many women must feel the sudden inconsistency with all that has gone before and an obvious point where the challenge of the Community Study has not even been recognised, let alone met. At one moment we are 'included in' and then relegated to a commentary. From this point on the text proceeds to talk of the all male ordained ministry of tradition. The question of the ordination of women to the priesthood is dismissed in a very carefully balanced commentary describing the positions of those churches that do, and those that do not, ordain women.

141. Later she says:

> It will be a test of the strength of the ecumenical movement whether the experience of those churches which do ordain women can be brought more centrally into the debate as we seek to get hold of our common Tradition. This will be a test of whether the methodological challenges of the Community Study have been taken seriously. Whether the churches can find agreement in the essentials of faith and allow a difference of practice over the ordination of women is a vital question asked by the Community Study. BEM gives no lead here. This is crucial not only for women but for the future visible unity of the Church.

142. The 'cautious retreat' described by Mary Tanner appears to have owed much to the increasing involvement of the Orthodox and their nervousness at any reference to women's ordination in ecumenical texts.

Relationships with other Communions

Old Catholic Churches (GS Misc 88, paras.106-113)

143. The present situation remains as in 1978: Anglican/Old Catholic intercommunion has been terminated in North America but not in Europe. So far as the Polish National Catholic Church is concerned, Prime Bishop

Zielinski has retired and been succeeded by Bishop Francis C. Rowinski. In November 1983, the first meeting of an official North American Working Group between the Episcopal Church USA and the PNCC took place.

The question of the effect of women ordained abroad being permitted to officiate in the Church of England on the relationship of full communion with the Old Catholics is being discussed in September 1984 by the International Bishops Conference. Meanwhile the Archbishop of Utrecht, having consulted the standing committee of that Conference, believes that the churches of Western Europe would not regard the Women Ordained Abroad Measure as a threat to full communion. The reaction of the Eastern European Churches and the PNCC in the USA is reticent or negative respectively.

Meanwhile, the Old Catholics in Germany are reported to have ordained women as deacons and in Switzerland are moving towards opening the diaconate to women.

144. An Old Catholic voice on the subject was heard from Fr. Nickel, at a meeting at Assisi in 1975:

> Our close association and innumerable joint meetings would inevitably entail the introduction of women clergy into our own church. The problem may be summed up in our case as placing before us the following alternative: (i) either it is a matter of substance requiring us to give notice to bring intercommunion to an end; (ii) or else it is purely a matter of procedure, in which case we should expedite the ordination of women into our own Church.

He pleaded for a Commission of Anglicans, Old Catholics, Orthodox and Roman Catholics to undertake a thorough investigation of the theological aspect of this question. 'No Catholic Church should make a unilateral attempt to introduce the ordination of women as priests and bishops in the absence of substantial agreement between the denominations' (Quoted in Ecumenical Review, July 1977. p.248) (see also Chapter VI)

Roman Catholic Church (GS 104. paras.280-294 and GS Misc 88, paras.114-129)

145. ACC4, in that part of its section on Unity concerned with relationships with the Roman Catholic Church, said:

> (d) The ordination of women
>
> A difficulty which arises from the Anglican side is the ordination of women. In receiving the report of the Anglican-Roman Catholic Consultation on the Ordination of Women to the Priesthood, commonly called the *Versailles Report,* we are aware of the grave obstacle this matter places in the way of reconciliation. *Versailles* was a Consultation and not a Commission and its report should not be understood as suggesting that the Roman Catholic Church might lightly change either its official attitude or practice. We note that the Consultation saw some

grounds for hope for reconciliation in sacramental fellowship in two ways: (1) the status of the question in the Roman Catholic Church; and (2) the intention of the member Churches of the Anglican Communion which ordain women not to depart from the traditional understanding of aspostolic ministry. (ACC-4 Report, p.9)

146. The Statement on Ministry and Ordination from the Anglican-Roman Catholic International Commission published in 1973, had nothing to say on the ordination of women but the Elucidation of that Statement, published in 1979, includes this paragraph:

Ordination of Women

5 Since the publication of the Statement there have been rapid developments with regard to the ordination of women. In those churches of the Anglican Communion where canonical ordinations of women have taken place, the bishops concerned believe that their action implies no departure from the traditional doctrine of the ordained ministry (as expounded, for instance, in the Statement). While the Commission realizes that the ordination of women has created for the Roman Catholic Church a new and grave obstacle to the reconciliation of our communions (cf. Letter of Pope Paul VI to Archbishop Donald Coggan, 23 March 1976, AAS 68), it believes that the principles upon which its doctrinal agreement rests are not affected by such ordinations; for it was concerned with the origin and nature of the ordained ministry and not with the question who can or cannot be ordained. Objections, however substantial, to the ordination of women are of a different kind from objections raised in the past against the validity of Anglican Orders in general.

(*The Final Report of the Anglican-Roman Catholic International Commission* — CTS/SPCK 1982, p.44)

The ordination of women is, however, on the agenda of ARCIC II. The second part of its main mandate is in the wording of the Archiepiscopal/Papal Common Declaration of 29 May 1982 'To study all that hinders the mutual recognition of the ministries of our communions.' This will involve the old question of Anglican Orders and the newer question of the ordination of women, but both in the context of the reconciliation of the Churches.

147. Brief reference was made in GS Misc 88, paras.125-126 to the Versailles Consultation. Its report, together with a covering letter from Bishop Howe (Secretary General of the ACC), was made available to General Synod members in time for the November 1978 debate (GS Misc 85 and 85a). It is reproduced in Appendix II.

148. In a speech to the General Synod in February 1978, Cardinal Hume said:

May I suggest that we must not only listen to each other, but together listen to what the Spirit is saying. There is an ancient practice in the Church of God, whereby the faith, and its formulation, tradition and ministries are matters to be decided in consultation with other local Churches. Now that our dialogue is progressing, and as we move in the direction of closer collaboration on the basis of this mutual communion between the Churches, it would — to take one important example — be a matter for deep concern were the Anglican Communion to proceed further with the ordination of women without taking very seriously the position of the Roman Catholic Church, our brothers of the Orthodox Churches and of the Old Catholic Churches regarding so momentous a change.

For Archbishop Coggan's subsequent conversations with Cardinal Hume, see his statement to Synod, February 1979, in Appendix I. See also Archbishop Runcie's answer to Canon Rhymes in Chapter I.

149. It would seem that while a number of Roman Catholic scholars in Europe and in North America have voiced the opinion that the ordination of women would be possible and criticism has been made of the arguments used in the Declaration (*Inter insigniores*), there has so far been no sign of any change in the position of the *magisterium* in Rome, nor so it seems, in the views of the great majority of Roman Catholic Bishops, though some may regard it as a possibility, open for discussion in the future.

Orthodox Churches (GS 104, paras.277-279 and GS Misc 88, paras.130-143)

150. *ACC4* in that part of its section on Unity concerned with the Orthodox said:

Undoubtedly the ordination of women in some Anglican Churches has deeply shaken the confidence of the Orthodox in the seriousness of Anglican resolve towards unity with them. This is illustrated in the *Athens Statement* (1978) of the Anglican-Orthodox Joint Doctrinal Discussions. But the measure of their shock is also the measure of their affection. In spite of the seriousness of this difficulty we hope that Anglican-Orthodox relations may increase in significance in the future, particularly in the countries of the Orthodox *diaspora as those communities mature in a common culture alongside other Christian traditions. We also note with interest the beginnings of official pan-Orthodox-Roman Catholic dialogue and recognize the importance of this in the healing of the split between Rome and Constantinople.*

Against the above background we welcome the achievement of the Anglican-Orthodox Joint Doctrinal Discussions as expressed in the *Moscow Agreed Statement* of 1976. With the 1978 Lambeth Conference (LCR 35.2) we hope the dialogue will continue fruitfully and endorse its suggestion of the promotion of regional groups.

Resolution 2: Anglican-Orthodox Relations

The Council re-affirms its commitment to Anglican-Orthodox dialogue and calls for the continuance of the Anglican-Orthodox Joint Doctrinal Discussions at the official and international level. *ACC-4* p.4.

The Report of the special meeting of the Anglican Orthodox Joint Doctrinal Commission (held in Athens July 1978) was referred to, and quoted from, in

GS Misc 88 paras.140-141. It was circulated to Synod members in its entirety as GS Misc 86. The relevant part is reproduced in Appendix III. (See also Archbishop Coggan's statement to Synod, February 1979, in Appendix I)

151. The meeting of the Commission in 1984 commented as follows:

We have failed to reach agreement concerning the possibility, or otherwise, of the ordination of women to the priesthood. The Orthodox affirm that such ordination is impossible, since it is contrary to Scripture and Tradition. With this some Anglicans agree, while others believe that it is possible, and even desirable at the present moment, to ordain women as priests. There are, however, many related issues that we have not so far examined in any detail, particularly the following: how we are to understand the distinction within humanity between man and woman; what is meant by sacramental priesthood, and how this is related to the unique high priesthood of Christ and to the royal priesthood of all the baptised; what, apart from the sacramental priesthood, are the other forms of ministry within the church.

Information Concerning Specific Churches

CHURCHES IN GREAT BRITAIN AND IRELAND

Church of Scotland (GS 104, para. 246 and GS Misc 88, para.78)

152. As at 31 December 1983 there were 1451 ministers serving the Pastoral Charges of the Church of Scotland: this number will have increased slightly through recent ordination but is unlikely to exceed 1500. Fifty of these ministers are women. Thirty-nine women are in parishes (of which four are held on a Terminable Basis), four are in some kind of Community Ministry, and one each in Service Overseas, Hospital Chaplaincy, the University of Edinburgh and the Church's Department of Education. Three are currently unemployed.

153. There are fifteen Probationers, that is to say women who have completed their University Course, been licensed to preach but have not yet been ordained, (about ten of these are not yet eligible for ordination since they are in the normal Probationary Period which follows licensing). There are 23 women in training for the ministry, including those already accepted for training and expected to complete their course in 1987, out of a total of 180. Women therefore represent 3 per cent of the total ministry but 13 per cent of the candidates in training.

154. Women do not experience particular difficulty in obtaining a call, except in so far as many women ministers, being married women, may not be mobile. The husband's job may require residence in a particular area so it

may simply not be possible to leave their present home and move to the Manse of the Charge. Particular difficulty seems to have been experienced where both husband and wife are ministers: in only one case are both husband and wife Ministers of Parishes close enough together to enable them to live in one Manse. However, in two cases, Minister married couples both occupy specialist posts.

155. There does seem to be some difficulty for a woman in obtaining a *second* charge. One woman has in fact occupied three Parishes, and another has gone from a Parish to Service Overseas. The remainder seem to have remained in their first charge, perhaps because of reduced mobility or even an enhanced 'stick-ability'.

Baptist Union of Great Britain and Ireland (GS 104, para.246 and GS Misc 88, para.69)

156. There are currently fifty-eight Baptist women ministers. Of these, eleven are retired and three are not in pastoral charge. Thirty-nine of the remaining forty-four are in the pastorate of local churches, the other six: Chaplain in Birmingham, Hon Chaplain Royal Navy, the Association Secretary for Lancashire and Chesire, Baptist Missionary Society Candidates' Secretary, BCC Youth Secretary and Lecturer at Heythrop Roman Catholic College. In addition, five of those in the pastorate of local churches hold, or have held, other posts of particular responsibility. One is Chairman of the Ministerial Recognition Committee, another is a Baptist representative on the Board of the BCC Division of Ecumenical Affairs, yet another is Secretary to the Baptist Peace Fellowship. Two, who have held posts at denominational level, (Secretary for Baptist Women's Work and Home Mission Promotion Office), have returned to the pastorate. There are three women ministers each in Birmingham and Coventry and two each in Alvechurch, Bristol and West Ham.

Methodist Church in England, Scotland and Wales
(GS 104, paras. 248-254 and GS Misc 88, paras.72-75)

157. The Methodist Church reports that it does not keep any figures about the number of ministers who are male or female. There are six women Superintendents.

Moravian Church (GS Misc 88, para.76)

158. Of the twenty-four ministers in the Moravian Church in Britain, three are women and there is one woman in training.

United Reformed Church (GS Misc 88, para.77 see also para.70 for the Churches of Christ, the major part of which has now united with the URC).

159. The URC has 165 women ministers of whom about 100 are active (there are about 800 active ministers in all). However none of the women are in charge of city centre churches, a matter concerning which the church leadership is raising questions.

SOME EUROPEAN CHURCHES

Church of Finland (GS Misc 88, paras.84-87)

160. In May 1984, the proposal to admit women to the ministry of the Church of Finland did not gain the three-quarters majority necessary to amend the Ecclesiastical Act, and it therefore failed. During the debate, which lasted a day and a half, Archbishop John Vikström spoke strongly in favour. The voting in the 108 member Synod was as follows: 73 in favour, 32 against and 3 abstentions. The bishops voted in favour by 6 to 2, the clerical members by 16 to 14, and the lay representatives by 48 to 16. All the 22 women members voted in favour as did the Government ministers who are *ex-officio* members.

Church of Sweden (GS 104, paras. 255-276 and GS Misc 88, paras.90-93)

161. In January 1984, there were 500 women priests (with subsequent ordinations there are now about 515-520) out of a total of about 3000 clergy, making 16-17 per cent. Thirty of these women are Rectors (Kyrkoherde).

162. Recently, the old 100 member Kyrkomöte (Church Assembly) has been replaced by a new 231 member Kyrkomöte. Bishops have a right to sit in this but have no vote unless elected by popular election. (It should be noted that the Swedish Kyrkomöte has never had anything comparable to our voting by Houses.)

163. When the 1958 decision to ordain women was taken, a conscience clause was attached to the law. This was as follows:

1. That a bishop should not be obliged to ordain a woman as a priest against his religiously grounded conviction.
2. That a priest should not be bound to perform in his ministry such tasks as would obviously violate his conscience because of the convictions that he holds on the question of the ordination of women.
3. That the priestly vows would not be interpreted to mean that someone who is an opponent of women priests cannot take them. (Unofficial translation).

In 1978 a consultative group met: it was drawn from both sides, and consisted of three bishops, three priests (one of whom was a woman), and six laymen, under the chairmanship of Archbishop Sundby, to consider the conscience clause in the prevailing circumstances. At the same time, a Parliamentary Committee considered the matter and there was a Government investigation. In the end, the 1958 law was simply abolished and therefore the law of equality between man and woman applied to the priestly profession as to any other. This rests on the 1975 fundamental, or constitutional, law and the 1979 law on equality of opportunity in employment.

164. The controversy referred to in GS Misc 88, para.92 has continued. The debate is not only over the question of women priests: it is also concerned with other matters, such as the Church-State relationship, and the question whether or not the present position, whereby a Swede is automatically registered at birth as a member of the Church of Sweden, if either parent were registered as a member, should continue, or be replaced by baptism as the basis for membership. The desire for some reform of Church State relationships and/or change in the basis of membership is by no means confined to those opposed to women priests. The new Kyrkomöte has set up a group to work on the question of the basis of Church membership and this has recently received a report from a theological commission set up by the Bishops' meeting, entitled 'Baptism and Church Membership', which has come out in favour of baptism as the basis for membership. Archbishop Bertil Werkström and almost all the bishops are reported to be in favour of this. However, a number of those who are concerned for renewal within the Swedish Church and who are critical of various aspects of Swedish church life, including the ordination of women, have formed a Free Synod: the chairman is Deaconess Maud Ohlson.

UNITED CHURCHES IN INDIA AND PAKISTAN (GS Misc 88, para.102)

Church of North India (GS Misc 88, para.102)

165. One woman was ordained in 1981 and there are currently two women presbyters of the CNI, one an Indian and the other an expatriate. It is left to each diocese to decide whether or not to ordain women.

Church of South India (GS Misc 88, paras.104-105)

166. The CSI now has four women presbyters. It is reported that there could be more but not all congregations would accept them.

Church of Pakistan

167. It is impossible at present to ordain women in a Muslim State.

A Conscience Clause

168. Reference to the sections on the Church of Canada (Chapter IV) and the Church of Sweden (Chapter V) as well as the section on Proposals for a Covenant (Chapter I) give some indication of problems that can arise in the area of the conscience clause (The Episcopal Church in the USA has a conscience clause from its House of Bishops. The Church of New Zealand has no conscience clause and it is recognised that when the one Bishop who will not ordain women retires, there will be no more bishops who will not do so in that country.)

169. Two questions, which can be easily overlooked, need to be borne in mind in the drafting of such a clause.

(i) Is the conscience clause to apply only to those clergy who are already in office, (or perhaps in training for the ministry), when the legislation is passed? Or is it to be a permanently available option to those who will enter the ministry at a later date? A variant of this relates to the episcopate: Once a Church/Province has accepted that women may be ordained to priesthood, ought a man to become a bishop who will not ordain women?

(ii) What is to happen if women priests feel that *their* rights of conscience are being denied by the exercise of the rights of conscience by another? What is the effect on a woman priest if her bishop asks her to stay away from an ordination because one of the men deacons to be ordained does not approve of the ordination of women?

170. While the Churches' Council for Covenanting was dealing with a somewhat different situation (though in many ways analogous to that concerning Women Ordained Abroad), the section on the meaning of 'Conscientious Reservation' seems important enough to be reproduced here.

The Meaning of 'Conscientious Reservation'

As we have begun our work it has seemed to us important to try to state how we understand the meaning of 'conscientious reservation', its theological basis and scope.

Negatively, the provision for 'conscientious reservation' does not imply that the matters in question are regarded as relatively unimportant; on the contrary they are matters which involve strong conviction about truth and error.

Positively, we understand the matter as follows:

(a) The matters in question are matters on which Christians hold contrary opinions with deep conviction, seeing them as part of their faithfulness to the Gospel.

(b)   But Christians find themselves called to acknowledge that those who hold opinions which they believe to be in error are nevertheless in Christ, live by the grace of God and bring forth the fruit of the Spirit.

(c)   Consequently they are unable to refuse communion with those whom God has accepted but are bound to remain in fellowship with them.

(d)   This fellowship does not exclude, but positively requires, a continuing and vigorous attempt, speaking the truth in love, to persuade the other of his error and to convince him or her of the truth.

(e)   Both parties are required to remain open to the possibility of new perspectives which may change their opinions.

(f)   'Rights of conscience' must always be exercised reciprocally; those who claim these rights must be particularly careful to ensure that they are also according them to others.

In summary, the matter of conscientious reservation must be understood entirely within the doctrine of the grace of God to sinners who may be and are in error but are nevertheless accepted in Christ.

(The Failure of the English Covenant, Appendix II, p.34)

VI WHAT IS THE DEBATE ABOUT? THE ORDINATION OF WOMEN, OR. . . .?

171. We have already seen in chapter II that debate upon the ordination of women often turns on some previous question. All of us operate with assumptions on a whole range of issues and we are not always aware that our own assumptions are not necessarily shared by others. Some of the fundamental issues on which there is disagreement were considered in GS 104, chapter III, 'Preliminary Considerations': Differing views on the Nature of Biblical Authority; Attitudes to Tradition; Ministry, Priesthood and Ordination; the Roles of Men and Women. In this chapter we are concerned with two particular issues: Ministry and Priesthood, and Authority in the Church. The second issue is considered in relationship to authority within the Anglican Communion and authority within the world Church, both of which raise questions of ecclesiastical decision-making. But first we consider the ways in which changes in the expression or understanding of doctrines which do not at first sight seem to be connected with the ordination of women debate, may, nevertheless, have a profound effect upon it.

The Inter-relationship of Doctrines

172. This inter-relationship and the effect of changes in understanding or emphasis in one area on another is considered by the Bishop of Salisbury (Rt Rev J.A. Baker) in his essay 'Carried about by every wind' in the Doctrine Commission's Report, *Believing in the Church* (SPCK, 1981). Noting that 'the various individual topics of Christian belief are related to one another at . . . many levels and in . . . a number of ways', he looks at three examples, each of which involves the Eucharist. Of one of these he says:

> A third aspect of the interplay of doctrines is that of the effect developments in one area have on another. This can be well illustrated from the doctrines of the Eucharist and the ordained ministry. The increasing emphasis on the Eucharist as sacrifice naturally reinforced the use of the term 'priest' to denote those ordained to celebrate it. The threefold ministry of bishop, priest and deacon was presented as the Christian fulfilment of the Old Testament high priest, priest and Levite (Cyprian, died 258). The growing importance of the Eucharist as the heart of Christian devotion helped to reduce the diaconate to a mere stage on the way to priesthood, and even, in Catholic theology, to blur the distinctiveness of the episcopal order. At the Reformation, therefore, not surprisingly the question whether to keep or reject the title of 'priest' was a key issue of conscience. A church which, like the Church of England, retained the term seemed to many to have jibbed at complete scriptural reform, however carefully it redefined its eucharistic teaching. Seventeenth-century Anglican piety (Herbert, Taylor, Ken)

went far to give fresh content of a pastoral kind to the idea of priesthood, in keeping with the 'reasonable, holy and lively sacrifice' of 'ourselves, our souls and bodies'. But the eucharistic altar and priestly sacrifice were still there in the general Christian background, and with the Tractarian Movement revived within the Church of England a conception of priesthood whose exponents soon came perforce to look to Roman Catholicism in various forms for authoritive guidance.

This divergence within the Church of England, primarily eucharistic in origin, has now created an impasse in the doctrine of ministry on two key matters which could make it impossible for that church to move as a united body into closer relations with any other. First, the conviction that the ministries of the Free Churches are not 'priestly' in intention, in the sense we have described, means that for a substantial minority of Church of England members some gesture implying supplementary ordination of Free Church ministers is indispensable before there can be mutual recognition of ministries. For others any such ingredient would be as totally unacceptable as it would be for the Free Church ministers themselves. The position of the former group is reinforced by another consideration: any other attitude to Free Church ministries could be held to undermine the point they feel it vital to make in discussions with the Roman Catholic Church, that Church of England ministerial order is truly priestly in a Catholic sense, and that therefore there is no need for the Church of Rome to insist on any kind of reordination in the case of Anglicans.

The second matter is that of the ordination of women. The opposition to this within the Church of England has numerous strands, but only one need concern us here. This is the stress on the ordained ministry as a 'priesthood'. The question, 'Can women be priests?' is the preferred battleground, and the use of the word 'priests' here is very far from a neutral denotation of the second degree of holy orders. Women ordained in the Free Churches, it is argued, though they preside at the Lord's Supper, are not ordained to the priesthood, because the Eucharist for them is not a sacrifice. Hence, too, the polemical use of the term, 'priestesses', differentiating in the light of the history of cults between the pagan religions, which allowed women to serve the altars, and the Jewish, which did not. A study of the controversial literature shows clearly that the conviction that women priests would be an impermissible development of doctrine is in part, at any rate, a manifestation in other guise of the unresolved Anglican argument about the Eucharist, carrying one side of this back to very early Christian speculations about the Eucharist as a replacement for the sacrificial cultus of the old Israel. Another related aspect, peculiarly significant for some Anglicans, is the so-called 'iconic' theory of the priesthood. The celebrant at the Eucharist is an 'icon' of Christ, the true High Priest, as he presided at the Last Supper. This is, in part, the logical conclusion of the western theory of the Eucharist, which sees the consecration of the elements as accomplished by the words of institution: Christ, present in his risen power, brings about what he first gave at the table in the upper room. Naturally, from this a line of argument follows that the one who represents Christ should be an image of him, not female but male. We do not here pass any judgement on the theological quality of this mental picture of the Eucharist; the purpose of mentioning it is simply to show how assumptions about the Eucharist exert the very strongest effect on discussion about the ministry. It is perhaps worth pointing out, however, the various factors which converge to give force to this approach. The prayer of consecration in the 1662 book means something very different when used in the spirit of a Catholic ethos of the priest as sacrificer from its sense and feel in the framework of Cranmer's theology. In the former case the prominence and critical importance of the institution narrative do indeed favour an understanding of the priest as acting the part of Christ. The recent widespread adoption of the westward position for the celebrant has intensified this interpretation, where it exists, because the priest visually and tellingly occupies the place of Christ in the traditional artistic representations of the Last Supper. When approaching such a tangled subject as the debate over the ordination of women, it is as well to bear in mind that some of the most important issues are not specifically about the role of women at all, but about the Eucharist. If we are asked to assess, for instance, whether the ordination of women is a legitimate development of Christian doctrine, we need to be clear *which* doctrines we are in truth talking about.

173. This long extract is included because it illustrates in one particular way the theme of this section, namely the way in which apparently unrelated issues come to affect one another. Our task is to understand this in relation to the question of the ordination of women. (For further consideration of ministry, see the next section, and for the concept of the priest as the icon of Christ, see Chapter VII).

The Nature of Priesthood and Ministry

174. 'The accepted background and tradition of minisry is now being challenged in almost every Church as a result of the study of the New Testament and of early Church history, as well as by changes in the patterns of society and by new ecumenical experience. . . . Some of the answers given are so radical that they call in question the very existence of a special or ordained ministry.' (GS 104, paras. 51 and 52. See also GS 104 paras.116-118, for a critical view of any attempt to ground opposition to the ordination of women to priesthood on a reading of New Testament evidence concerning 'apostolic ministry' or 'eucharist').

175. One such challenge is to be found in Richard Hanson's *Christian Priesthood Examined,* (Lutterworth, 1979).

No Ministers in the Primitive Church

As we approach the subject of Christian priesthood, it is first necessary to face the question of Christian ministry generally. When we speak today of Christian ministers and the Christian ministry we invariably mean ministry as the great majority of Christian denominations know it today, that is a ministry consisting of officers appointed to fill official posts in the church who have themselves succeeded to officers filling these posts before them and who will in course of time be succeeded by other officers who will fill their posts when they retire or leave or die. This concept of ministry, which I shall call 'official ministry' is usually applied to full-time permanent ministers, but it can also be applied to part-time permanent ministers and even to those who occupy a ministry for a defined period and then leave it. The essential point about this type of ministry is that it consists of an office to be filled, to which officials can succeed; also that it is either permanent or for a determined time, not occasional or *ad hoc*. This definition of ministry applies to almost all forms of ministry filled by Christian ministers today, whether they are popes or archbishops or bishops or priest or deacons or pastors or just ministers, whether they claim apostolic succession or scriptural authority or not, whether they are paid or unpaid, established or free, male or female, whether they wear clerical collars or do not, whether they call themselves Catholic or Reformed, apostolic or evangelical.

It must first be understood that in the earliest age of the church no such ministry as this existed, and therefore that no such ministry, in any of its forms, can justly claim that it was instituted by Christ or his apostles, nor that it has any particular right to call itself exclusively scriptural. (pp.8-9)

Later Hanson says: 'No christian priesthood is to be found in the New Testament. There is in fact no solid evidence that anyone thinks of christian ministers as priests until after the year 200 AD.' (Ibid, p.35) He adds:

This is not to say that an apostolic ministry does not exist and that a ministry may not be either scriptural or non-scriptural, but it is maintained that it cannot be so in the senses outlined above. It is possible to argue that one or more particular forms of ministry express and realize the apostolic mission of the church and are therefore in that sense apostolic, reproducing the apostles' mission and activity. (Ibid, p.90)

He goes on to say: 'The church developed the official ministry because it needed the official ministry.' (Ibid, p.93) A somewhat different, but equally critical picture is found in Edward Schillebeeckx's *Ministry: a case for change* (English Translation, SCM Press, 1981): 'Apart from apostleship or the 'apostolate', the Christian communities did not receive any kind of church order from the hands of Jesus when he still shared our earthly history' (Ibid, p.5)

176. Among the questions at issue are such matters as: can bishops be said to derive directly from the Twelve? What is the meaning of the terms priest and priesthood when used for Christian ministers, and how do they relate to Old Testament conceptions of ministry? Is it any longer possible to assert unequivocally with the Preface to the Ordinal in the Book of Common Prayer: 'It is evident unto all men diligently reading holy Scripture and ancient Authors, that from the Apostles' time there have been these Orders of Ministers in Christ's Church; Bishops, Priests and Deacons,' at least in the developed sense that the Ordinal understands these Offices?

177. Is there such a thing as a common mind of the Church of England on such matters concerning ministry? Whatever debates may take place among scholars, the Church of England does not normally deal with such matters at

an official level unless, and until, fundamental questions are raised, usually because there are practical consequences. Thus, in the last decades, the Church has been obliged to give some consideration to this because of what is happening in three areas: in the field of Christian unity, the search for a closer relationship with the Roman Catholic Church, and the attempts to find a way of reconciling or integrating ministries with certain English Free Churches; in the emergence of non-stipendiary and local ordained ministry; and in the ordination of women. All of these raise questions as to the mind of the Church of England on priesthood and ministry.

With the first two of these particularly in mind, and in an attempt to provide a Theology of Ordination, the Faith and Order Advisory Group produced two reports for debate in General Synod: *The Theology of Ordination and the Integration of Ministries,* GS 212, 1974 and *The Theology of Ordination,* GS 281, 1975.

178. Since this last report is not readily available it may be useful to reproduce an excerpt from its section on Priestly Ministry.

13. The fundamental Christian ministry is that of Christ himself. His self-emptying and self-offering alone reconcile the world to God, and there can be no Christian ministry or mediation apart from him.

14. Yet he chooses to involve men in his work of reconciliation (John 17.18f; 20.21; *cf* I Cor. 3.9). From the time of St Paul, the Church has understood itself to be blessed by certain spiritual gifts or graces (charismata) which are not all given to all Christians, nor are they the private possessions of those who receive them: rather are they graces given to certain individuals to be exercised to the benefit of all (*cf* e.g. I Cor. 12).

15. As the early Church (for whatever reasons) became more concerned with its own organisation, it significantly re-emphasised the fact of ministry being the gift of Christ or of his Spirit, bestowed upon those whom he had chosen. *Cf* Eph. 4.7-11 (a more 'institutional' list than I Cor. 12); I Tim. 4.14; II Tim. 1.6; I Clement 42-44. None of the books in the New Testament uses explicitly sacerdotal language of the ministry, but Hippolytus (c AD 200) uses it of the work of the bishop: he is 'to feed thy flock and serve as thine high priest (αρχιερατευειν) . The subsequent development of this terminology for the ministry of bishops and presbyters is well known, being the result partly of the influence of Old Testament types and partly of an association with the priestly role of Christ. The sixteenth century reformers consciously rejected this sacerdotal language, but they in no way relinquished their belief in a distinctive ministry. Thus the Second Helvetic Confession (1556) says, 'The priesthood and the ministry are very different from one another. . . For the Lord himself did not appoint any priests. . . but ministers who may preach and administer the sacraments'. (Ch. 18).' These historical texts may be compared with two modern statements from different ecclesiastical traditions:

'Presbyters. . . are consecrated to preach the Gospel, shepherd the faithful and

celebrate the divine worship as the true priests (sacerdotes) of the new Covenant.'
(*Lumen Gentium, para.28)*[2]
'The essential and specific function of the special ministry is: to assemble and build up the Christian community, by proclaiming and teaching the word of God, and presiding over the liturgical and sacramental life of the eucharistic community.' (*The Ordained Ministry in Ecumenical Perspective,* para. 15).[3] These quotations suggest there is a real danger of our being imprisoned by words. When titles such as priest and minister are 'unpacked' they are found to represent very similar ideas of a distinctive aspect of the life of the Church. Put in another way, if there is a distinctive ministry, then primitive Christianity, the sixteenth century reformers and the main strands of Christian theology today seem to be in substantial agreement about the basic essentials of it.

16. A related problem derives from the overstressing of sacerdotal language in relation to the ministry. This has led on the one hand to complications over the nature of 'sacrifice' etc., and on the other to a dubious linking together — through the catchword 'priest' — of themes which have no original connection. For example, the readers of I Peter are told, 'You are a chosen race, a royal priesthood, a consecrated nation'. The contexts of this text, of Exodus 19.6 (from which it is quoted) and of related passages in Revelation all emphasise the *corporate* nature of the concept here involved. The true Israel is a priestly *body* in that it enlightens the world concerning God; the Christian interpretation will include the sense in which, because the Church is the Body of Christ, this corporate priesthood is derived from Christ. But this is not to be confused with the distinctive charismata associated with the ministry which, as was seen above, are bestowed upon *individuals.*

17. Three elements in the traditional Christian use of the language of priesthood are thus discernible:
(i)   The unique priesthood of Christ himself.
(ii)   The corporate priesthood of the whole Church.
(iii)   The priesthood of those ordained to the proclamation of the word, the administration of the sacraments and the pastoral care of the faithful.

While it is true that ministers of word and sacrament are not excluded from the corporate priesthood, and that all Christian priesthood must derive from Christ, it is not possible to equate these three elements nor even to move without great care from speaking of one to speaking of another. While Christian piety has used these elements to enrich each other, it is necessary theologically to keep them distinct. (GS 281, pp.6-8)

[1] *Reformed Confessions, pp.271-2.*
[2] *Documents of Vatican II, p.53.*
[3] Modern Ecumenical Documents on the Ministry, p.33.

179. Appendix 2 to GS 281, *Ministry in the New Testament,* is concerned with two problems:

(i) The divergence of scholarly opinion concerning the accuracy, historicity and purpose of the New Testament documents.

(ii) The difficulty of moving from description to prescription in matters of Church order.

180. On the second, of these, it has this to say:

A cursory reading of the New Testament reveals a variety of titles and functions, together with a number of different pictures of Church life and structure (or lack of it). Pre-critical students of scripture worked on the assumption that the texts were capable of harmonisation; the basic model to which the others were assimilated may have differed according to the ecclesiastical leanings of the writer, but the premise of a single original ideal Church was common to all. A critical view of scripture does not preclude the possibility that the New Testament Church formed an ideal model which is recoverable and ought to be followed, but neither does it demand it. Consequently some recent scholarship has concentrated on the exploration of differences between the New Testament writers, with a view to accentuating rather than harmonising the discrepancies. As a result it has been claimed that the New Testament does itself represent a plurality of views about the Church and Church order.

The New Testament is the record — partial indeed but the best we have — of the proclamation of the Gospel of Jesus Christ. Journeyings, healings, sermons, visions, encounters, deaths, new life, great achievements, bitter disappointments — all are set down, and together they not only *record* the proclamation but actually *are* — for us — the proclamation of the Gospel. And inextricably bound up with this is the birth of the Church. The question is: how far can the *de*scriptions of the embryo and infant Church in the New Testament be taken as *pre*scriptions for the Church of our own day? Cyprian in the third century and Calvin in the sixteenth each attempted a straight reading of a Church Order off the pages of the New Testament: it is pertinent to ask whether such a procedure would be desirable today, even if it were possible.

Whatever picture of the New Testament Church emerges, the acceptance of a canon of scripture implies an acceptance of that picture as one fixed point to which reference must be made to test current ideas. Not to make such reference would be to cut ourselves off from our essential roots. But equally important is a recognition of the needs of the present day and also of the pattern of growth over the intervening period: without this the scriptural picture would be misleading and result in a denial of the true nature of both the New Testament and the Church as the agents for the proclamation of the Gospel to every generation. (GS 281 pp.29-30)

In fact neither GS 212 nor GS 281 refer at any point to the ordination of women, assuming perhaps that the debate then in progress on GS 104 obviated the need to do so. But one issue, which lay at the root of much of the contents of both Reports, namely to discover whether there is sufficient doctrinal agreement, particularly in respect of the ministry, to make effective negotiations with other churches possible, could be rephrased to apply also to the question of the ordination of women.

181. Reference can also be made to two Reports which, while not from the Church of England, involved members of this Church in their compilation: *The Final Report of the Anglican — Roman Catholic International Commission* (ARCIC), and *Baptism, Eucharist and Ministry.*

182. Much attention has been given to the ARCIC Statement on Ministry and Ordination, para.13 (originally published 1973):

The priestly sacrifice of Jesus was unique, as is also his continuing High Priesthood. Despite the fact that in the New Testament ministers are never called 'priests' (*hiereis*), Christians came to see the priestly role of Christ reflected in these ministers and used priestly terms in describing them. Because the eucharist is the memorial of the sacrifice of Christ, the action of the presiding minister in reciting again the words of Christ at the last supper and distributing to the assembly the holy gifts is seen to stand in a sacramental relation to what Christ himself did in offering his own sacrifice. So our two traditions commonly used priestly terms in speaking about the ordained ministry. Such language does not imply any negation of the once-for-all sacrifice of Christ by any addition or repetition. There is in the eucharist a memorial (*anamnesis*) of the totality of God's reconciling action in Christ, who through his minister presides at the Lord's Supper and gives himself sacramentally. So it is because the eucharist is central to the Church's life that the essential nature of the Christian ministry, however this may be expressed, is most clearly seen in its celebration; for, in the eucharist, thanksgiving is offered to God, the gospel of salvation is proclaimed in word and sacrament, and the community is knit together as one body in Christ. Christian ministers are members of this redeemed community. Not only do they share through baptism in the priesthood of the people of God, but they are — particularly in presiding at the eucharist — representative of the whole Church in the fulfilment of its priestly vocation of self-offering to God as a living sacrifice (Rom. 12.1). Nevertheless their ministry is not an extension of the common Christian priesthood but belongs to another realm of the gifts of the Spirit. It exists to help the Church to be 'a royal priesthood, a holy nation, God's own people, to declare the wonderful deeds of him who called (them) out of darkness into his marvellous light' (l Pet.2.9). *The Final Report,* pp.35/36

183. The Elucidation to this Report (1979) contains a further reflection on Priesthood:

2 In common Christian usage the term *priesthood* is employed in three distinct ways: the priesthood of Christ, the priesthood of the people of God, the priesthood of the ordained ministry.

The priesthood of Christ is unique. He is our High Priest who has reconciled mankind with the Father. All other priesthood derives from his and is wholly dependent upon it.

The priesthood of the whole people of God (1 Peter 2.5) is the consequence of incorporation by baptism into Christ. This priesthood of all the faithful (para. 7) is not a matter of disagreement between us. In a document primarily concerned with the ordained ministry, the Commission did not consider it necessary to develop the subject further than it has already done in the Statement. Here the ordained ministry is firmly placed in the context of the ministry of the whole Church and exists for the service of all the faithful.

The Statement (para.13) explains that the ordained ministry is called priestly principally because it has a particular sacramental relationship with Christ as High Priest. At the eucharist Christ's people do what he commanded in memory of himself and Christ unites them sacramentally with himself in his self-offering. But in this action it is only the ordained minister who presides at the eucharist, in which, in the name of Christ and on behalf of his Church, he recites the narrative of the institution of the Last Supper, and invokes the Holy Spirit upon the gifts.

The word *priesthood* is used by way of analogy when it is applied to the people of God and to the ordained ministry. These are two distinct realities which relate, each in its own way, to the high priesthood of Christ, the unique priesthood of the new covenant, which is their source and model. These considerations should be borne in mind throughout para. 13, and in particular they indicate the significance of the statement that the ordained ministry 'is not an extension of the common Christian priesthood but belongs to another realm of the gifts of the Spirit'.

In this as in other cases the early Church found it necessary for its understanding and exposition of the faith to employ terminology in ways in which it was not used in the New Testament. Today in seeking to give an account of our faith both our communions, in the interpretation of the Scriptures, take cognisance of the Church's growing understanding of Christian truth (cf. Authority I, paras.2, 3, and 15). (Ibid. pp.40-42)

184. On the matter of the Ordained Ministry and Priesthood, the *Lima Text* has this by way of Report and Commentary:

C. Ordained Ministry and Priesthood

17. Jesus Christ is the unique priest of the new covenant. Christ's life was given as a sacrifice for all. Derivatively, the Church as a whole can be described as a priesthood. All members are called to offer their being 'as a living sacrifice' and to intercede for the Church and the salvation of the world. Ordained ministers are related, as are all Christians, both to the priesthood of Christ, and to the priesthood of the Church. But they may appropriately be called priests because they fulfil a particular priestly service by strengthening and building up the royal and prophetic priesthood of the faithful through word and sacraments, through their prayers of intercession, and through their pastoral guidance of the community.

COMMENTARY (17)

The New Testament never uses the term 'priesthood' or 'priest' (*hiereus*) to designate the ordained ministry or the ordained minister. In the New Testament, the term is reserved, on the one hand, for the unique priesthood of Jesus Christ and, on the other hand, for the royal and prophetic priesthood of all baptized. The priesthood of Christ and the priesthood of the baptized have in their respective ways the function of sacrifice and intercession. As Christ has offered himself, Christians offer their whole being 'as a living sacrifice'. As Christ intercedes before the Father, Christians intercede for the Church and the salvation of the world. Nevertheless, the differences between these two kinds of priesthood cannot be overlooked. While Christ offered himself as a unique sacrifice once and for all for the salvation of the world, believers need to receive continually as a gift of God that which Christ has done for them. In the early Church the terms 'priesthood' and 'priest' came to be used to designate the ordained ministry and minister as presiding at the eucharist. They underline the fact that the ordained ministry is related to the priestly reality of Jesus Christ and the whole community. When the terms are used in connection with the ordained ministry, their meaning differs in appropriate ways from the sacrificial priesthood of the Old Testament, from the unique redemptive priesthood of Christ and from the corporate priesthood of the people of God. St Paul could call his ministry 'a priestly service of the gospel of God, so that the offering of the Gentiles may be acceptable by the Holy Spirit' (Rom. 15:16). (*Lima Text* p.23)

(For further extracts from both these Reports, see Chapter V.)

185. Resolution 21:8 of the 1978 Lambeth Conference asked 'that further discussions about the ordination of women be held within a wider consideration of the theological issues of ministry and priesthood.' Reflection on some of the quotations in this section and on the large amount of literature currently available on these issues suggests that such wider consideration is urgently necessary yet may not easily lead to a common Anglican mind. It is against this background that we turn to the questions concerning authority in the Church.

Authority in the Church and decision-making

186. It is impossible fully to consider so vast a subject in this report but there are two aspects of it which have become increasingly important in relation to the ordination of women. Has an Anglican Province the right to decide this matter on its own or should it wait for a common Anglican Communion decision? Has the Anglican Communion itself the right to decide such a matter or does it require an ecumenical decision? It is to these two issues that we now turn.

THE ANGLICAN COMMUNION AND AUTHORITY WITHIN THE COMMUNION: CAN ONE PROVINCE DECIDE?

187. When GS 104 was written in 1972 the only women to have been ordained priest in the Anglican Communion were in the diocese of Hong Kong. By the time of the 1978 debate, they had been joined by women priests in Canada, New Zealand and the USA, in each case after due synodical decision. Put in another way, between the reopening of the question of the ordination of women at the 1968 Lambeth Conference and the 1978 Lambeth Conference, the Anglican picture had radically changed. This has been regretted, even by those not opposed in principle: would it not have been better, it is said, for the Communion to move together or at least to take counsel together?

188. In his introductory speech at the 1978 Lambeth Conference Hearing on the Ordination of Women, Professor John Macquarrie considered this point. He posed the question: 'How much agreement should there be before such a major innovation as the ordination of women is implemented?' He turned to the question of a consensus and said: 'It cannot mean everyone

thinking alike. . . . A measure of pluralism is today an acceptable and healthy state of affairs within the Church. But sheer pluralism would mean the dissolution of the Church. The liberty of pluralism is possible only because there are wide areas of agreement. . . . The ordination of women to the priesthood and episcopate is such a novel step that it does seem to me to demand a large measure of consensus if it is not to provoke very deep division and even schism.'

189. Professor Macquarrie considered this requirement for consensus within a particular national or regional Church and continued:

But the question does arise whether on such an important and potentially divisive issue as the ordination of women to the priesthood, one should not look for a consensus beyond that of the national or regional Church. It is true of course that within the Anglican Communion, each constituent Church is autonomous. But I must confess that I am not much impressed with the idea of an autonomous Church. This is especially the case at a time when we hear a great deal of talk about collegiality, partnership, conciliarity, and so on. If these are not just empty words that are bandied about, if they stand for a real desire to share experience and decision-making, then each so-called autonomous Church ought to be in constant consultation with its sister Churches. On the particular matter with which we are concerned today, it would surely have been wise if individual Churches had deferred action until this Lambeth Conference of 1978.
(*Report of the Lambeth Conference 1978* pp.116-118)

190. A somewhat similar view from a different perspective was set out by Bishop John Howe, (Secretary-General of the Anglican Consultative Council) in an address to ACC-4. He noted that:

While belonging to a world-wide Communion is welcomed, Anglican Churches. . . have a capacity for isolationism – for becoming so occupied with their own affairs that they forget other Churches exist, or might reasonably be consulted. . . .there is little consultation or collaboration. Studies . . . on similar subjects tend to be repeated across the world and reports produced often without enquiry about similar work being done elsewhere, by Anglicans or by others. I think we were all helped to realise this limitation by the considerations of that major subject, the ordination of women to the priesthood. It was not in anyone's power to decide when the issue would become one that required decision, but had it been a few years later I believe more Churches would have been unwilling to be left largely on their own, and greater preliminary deliberation among the whole family, and ecumenically, would have been required and demanded. Only after that would the Churches individually have felt ready to make their decisions. The outcome might have been the same, but the procedure would have been more appropriate. (*Report of ACC-4,* 1979, p.71) (See also ACC-4, the 'Ecumenical Consequences of the Ordination of women', Chapter VI)

191. However, the Rt Rev. Barry Valentine, then Bishop of Rupert's Land in Canada, had this to say in his article on 'Women and the Ministry',

(*Today's Church and Today's World.* The Lambeth Conference 1978, Preparatory Articles).

> Questions as to whether the Anglican Communion or Provinces of it, or national churches within it, or synods or Houses of Bishops or the Lambeth Conference itself – are legitimately able to decide about the ordination of women and to act in the decision taken are clearly important because they concern the very unity of the Communion; but they must be seen as what they are and not as determining an issue which must surely be decided on other grounds. (pp:184-185)

And, as a Canadian Archbishop was to say in 1982, they did indeed consult and evidenced the discussion and resolution of ACC-1 at Limuru. (See GS 104, para.13)

192. This raises inevitably the question of authority within the Anglican Communion, its nature and where it may be found. Dr Coggan, then Archbishop of Canterbury, addressed this question in a speech to the 1978 Lambeth Conference, on authority in the Anglican Communion.

> We have been searching somewhat uneasily to find out where the centre of that authority is. . . . There are those who would say. . . that authority ought to be centred in the person of the Archbishop of Canterbury himself, but down the years the feeling against that has, I think rightly, been strong. It is not. . . .of the genius of Anglicanism to have at its head someone who is papal or patriarchal. . . .

> Is the answer then to rest with the Lambeth Conference? Again the answer has been, and again I think rightly, no. For, so far, we have insisted on saying that we are not a legislative body. We are what our title implies — a conference, a conferring body. We may sense a consensus and that is very important, but we do not legislate.

> Is the central authority of the Anglican Communion, then, to rest with the Anglican Consultative Council? Again I believe the answer is no. This, though a synodical body, consisting of bishops, priests, and laity, is not representative enough — anything like representative enough — of the whole world-wide 65 or 70 million of us.

193. Archbishop Coggan went on to consider the role of a Doctrine Commission in this but again did not see it 'as being the authoritive council of the Anglican Communion'. He concluded by hoping that the meetings of the Primates together with their close and intimate contact with the ACC would help. He concluded:

> We should, I believe, come to a common mind on main issues and we should avoid the danger of one Church, or two or three Churches, going off on their own without due consultation — at the same time maintaining the independence of the member Churches themselves. . . .

> I believe that on lines something like these — without a rigidity which would be foreign to our tradition — we should move towards a maturity in the exercise of authority which would be to the good of our Communion as a whole and might

well be the means through us of our making a contribution to the whole Catholic Church of God. (*Report of Lambeth Conference 1978,* pp.122-124)

194. When Archbishop Scott addressed the General Synod in July 1982 he said:

Some reflections on women ordained to the priesthood within the Anglican Communion. Here I am going to set forth some things very briefly and ask a question. Since no Anglican Province acted to ordain women to the priesthood until the Lambeth Conference had carefully discussed this possibility and until major Provinces had by majority vote expressed the view that there were no compelling theological reasons why women should not be ordained; since a number of Provinces of the Communion have, after careful study and consultation, acted canonically to ordain women to the priesthood, which means that the Anglican Communion includes women priests; since the Lambeth Conference in 1978 expressed the view that Provinces who have so acted, and Provinces which have not done so, are equally in good standing within our Communion; since there is no evidence in Provinces that have so acted that God has not chosen to use the ministries of women so ordained as efficacious ministries of Word and Sacrament: would it not be a more adequate expression of the Anglican understanding of 'full communion', of 'mutual recognition of ministry' and of 'dispersed authority' if Provinces which have not acted to ordain women to the priesthood were to recognise all of the priests of those Provinces which have, and, without prejudice to their own position, allow women validly and regularly ordained in their own Province, where so requested by diocesan bishops, to excercise their ministries of Word and Sacrament in settings where such an exercise would be welcomed? I do not mean this to be a loaded question, even though it may appear that way. I just pose the question.

THE ANGLICAN COMMUNION AND AUTHORITY WITHIN THE WORLD CHURCH: CAN ONE COMMUNION ACT ON ITS OWN?

195. Though this aspect of authority in decision-making seems to have featured more prominently in Synod debates than the inter-Anglican one, the two questions are of course related. Preaching in York Minster during the Halifax celebrations in January 1984, the Archbishop of York (Dr Habgood) said: 'The questions, "who can speak for the Church?" and "how far does that speaking for the Church rest on the consent of the faithful?" are to a very large extent the key ecumenical questions' (*One in Christ,* 1984, 2, p.154).

196. The Archbishop of Canterbury, Dr Runcie, speaking in the debate on Deaconess McClatchey's motion on Women Lawfully Ordained Abroad in July 1982, said that he had

regretted the way in which separate provinces of the Anglican Communion took independent action on the subject and believed that the stance of the Church of England was important, in fact, has been important in terms of our ecumenical dialogue with Rome and the Orthodox. But it is quite clear now, after a number of

67

years, that we belong to a Communion, some parts of which ordain women to the priesthood and others do not.

197. The Archbishop put the last point even more strongly when, in the debate in July 1984 on the draft Women Ordained Abroad Measure, he said:

It is clearer now that the ordination of women to the priesthood — like it or like it not — is almost certainly a permanent development in the ministry of at least some Anglican Churches.

198. This suggests that there are a number of different approaches to this question (apart, that is to say, from those who are firmly convinced that the ordination of women is not simply undesirable but in fact impossible).

199. One such approach has been set out by Canon Roger Greenacre in a paper published in *Irénikon* (1984/No. 2) (translation by Canon Greenacre):

Is not the crisis over the ordination of women to the priesthood, which risks tearing apart the unity of the Anglican Communion above all and before all else a problem of Anglican ecclesiology? Before the 19th Century such an evolution would have been unthinkable and the classical Anglican appeal to the Bible and the consensus of the undivided Church allowed no room for the possibility of developments of this nature which would have required the authoritative solution of totally new problems. Does not the admission of the possibility of women priests imply the admission also of the development of Christian doctrine in the sense in which Newman argued? A Church which considers itself a part of the *Una Sancta* — but only a part — can defend and reaffirm what has already been decided by ecumenical authority, but can it resolve alone a totally new question? Ought it not rather to confess its impotence in this field? This debate for us Anglicans is not therefore just a question about our anthropology or about our theology of the ministry but above all a question about authority in the Church and the limits of purely Anglican authority. It is essentially a question of ecclesiology.

200. In General Synod in the November 1983 debate on Women Ordained Abroad Canon Greenacre spoke of:

the one fundamental theological issue at stake: the issue of our theology of the Church and our understanding of authority, what authority the Church of England or any other Churches of the Anglican Communion have to decide this issue and act on it unilaterally.

The argument here is not the same as that which asks whether, for the sake of maintaining our relations of full communion with the Old Catholics, or of avoiding further obstacles in our dialogue with Rome and the East, we ought to decide this issue alone. It is more radical than that. It asks whether we can do it, whether we possess the authority from God to do it. Since the credentials of Anglicanism, as Bishop Michael Ramsey has told us, are its incompleteness, with the tension and travail and its very brokenness pointing through and beyond itself to the universal Church, our Anglican self-understanding will only allow us to see ourselves as a fragment of the one Catholic Church of Christ.

So we must inevitably ask: what are the limits to Anglican authority and what are the issues on which we have to say that we do not have the right to legislate on this alone? We can only act when there is a clear consensus in Christendom that this particular development in faith or order is a legitimate development we can all recognise as coming to us from the Holy Spirit of God.

(For a similar view from Archbishop Kok of Utrecht, see GS Misc 88, para.108. The full text of Archbishop Kok's letter is in GS Misc 53)

201. A second approach to this question is made by those who are not opposed in principle to the ordination of women—indeed who may see strong reasons in favour — but who attach greater importance to the quest for Christian unity, particularly with the Roman Catholic Church. One such view was put by Canon Rhymes (Southwark) in moving his amendment to the 1978 motion on the ordination of women. See chapter I.

When I ask in this amendment for a consensus of agreement I do not mean. . . .that we should wait until the Greek Orthodox Church decides to ordain women, which will probably be in about 2000 years, or until the Church of Rome decides to do so, but rather that we should wait until they come together with us and are able to say categorically that what we do in this respect, whether 'Yes' or 'No', is not going to affect the ultimate unity of catholic Christendom.

202. A modified form of this approach would be that of making serious dialogue with Roman Catholics, Old Catholics and Orthodox a precondition before a decision could be made, (see Professor Jones' amendment in the same debate, Chapter I), but not of requiring a consensus decision.

203. In Professor Macquarrie's 1978 Lambeth Conference speech already referred to he said:

One has also to ask the question of how the existence of women priests in Anglican Churches will affect our relations with Churches outside our own Communion. The major difficulty will arise with Rome and the Orthodox. It will be sad indeed if the promising *rapprochement* between Rome and Canterbury is halted or slowed down by the ordination of women priests in Anglican Churches. This may very well happen, and I hope we all realize that we may be paying a very high price for what we are doing. Yet perhaps it won't happen, and here I would appeal to the generosity and understanding of the Roman brethren in particular. If indeed, as I have claimed, women in the priesthood is a genuinely disputed question belonging to that peripheral area where pluralism is legitimate, is it not possible for our two Communions to continue to grow together on the basis of the many things that they have in common, while respecting differences of discipline on matters which surely do not make or unmake a Church? (*Report of the Lambeth Conference 1978*, p.119)

The question under debate is precisely whether women priests do belong to that 'peripheral area where pluralism is legitimate' or whether, as some would hold, it is not a matter of discipline (such as the legitimacy of a married clergy) but rather, as Rome and the Orthodox would claim, it is a question about the requirements for the valid celebration of a sacrament, and therefore a fundamental matter.

204. Others would suggest that the ordination of women is what the Archbishop of Canterbury has called (in his 1984 speech already quoted) 'a second order question which does not lie at the heart of faith.' The ecumenical question would then be, can other Churches so regard it, and, if not, can the Church of England tarry, and for how long, seeking a consensus? Perhaps the best articulation of the dilemma is posed by the remit of the Versailles Consultation: 'To what extent and in what ways Churches with women priests and Churches without women priests can be reconciled in sacramental fellowship?' (See also Chapter V and Appendix II). This is already a problem *within* the Anglican Communion which has not however led to the breaking of communion: can the Anglican Communion, which has women priests enter into communion with the Roman Catholic and Orthodox Churches which do not, or does it remain a specific barrier?

205. In moving resolution 21 of the 1978 Lambeth Conference (see GS Misc 88, para.29) the Bishop of Derby (Rt Rev. Cyril Bowles) said:

Concerning clause 7, strong representations have been made to us by the Roman Catholic Church, the Orthodox Churches, and the Old Catholic Churches. It would be most discourteous, to say the least, merely to go our own way and say nothing. We must go our own way when truth and loyalty to our own Communion demand this, but we are engaged in dialogue with two of these groups and have full communion with the third. This clause is an attempt to avoid rebuff, to state our own position, and at the same time to show some humbleness of mind. Therefore, we say, first of all, in section (a) of clause 7 that we are not merely making the best of a bad job. We are doing something much more positive than that. Here is an inherent part of our Anglican inheritance, the holding together of diversity within a unity of faith and worship. This is not something that was invented at the time of the Reformation and developed in subsequent centuries. It is something to be found in the New Testament itself, Christians respecting one another, sharing a common life, and accepting also a diversity of conviction on sundry matters. Section (b) makes clear what is being thought about when we refer to the ordination of women to the priesthood. Whether we believe it is right or wrong, we are not introducing something new. Those who have been ordained have been ordained into the historic ministry of the Church as the Anglican Communion has received it. In section (c) of this clause we make it clear that we still want to learn. We do not possess all the answers, but so long as Churches are disunited something is lacking of the fullness of catholicity, of the measure of the stature of the fullness of Christ. (*Report of the Lambeth Conference, 1978, p.121)*

A major part of the debate in this area seems concentrated on possible relationships of communion with the Roman Catholic and Orthodox Churches and our existing relationship of communion with the Old Catholic Churches. Others would wish to widen the debate and include at least the Lutheran Churches, and those Churches with whom we have been ecumenical conversations in these islands (the Church of Scotland and in the main English Free Churches).

207. In the New Zealand Church, the question of the ordination of women seems to have become a live issue when that Church was considering a Plan of Union and whether it could accept the women ministers of the other Churches. A report to the Christ Church Diocesan Synod in 1968 on the ordination of women put the dilemma thus:

> If we accept the ordination of women to the Sacred Ministry we may add to the division of world wide Christendom. If we do not we may perpetuate the divisions in the Christian Ministry in New Zealand
>
> (Quoted in Dr K.N. Booth, *Christianity in New Zealand.*)

208. This dilemma is similar to that experienced by the Churches' Council for Covenanting and is also reflected in the Report of the Anglican-Reformed International Commission (*God's Reign and our Unity,* SPCK/ St Andrew Press, 1984):

> It is clearly impossible for churches which exist in the same geographical area but which take different stands on this issue to enter into complete union. It is therefore an issue the solution of which cannot be postponed much longer. (pp.63-64)

209. It would appear that the conversations had particularly in mind the experience of the Churches' Council for Covenanting and this recalls the view expressed in *The Failure of the English Covenant* that, so long as the Church of England remains in a state of ambivalence over the ordination of women, it is probably 'un-unitable with'. (See also the comments of Father Nickel quoted in chapter V.)

210. Others would echo the words of the Orthodox Churchman quoted in GS 104, para. 279, 'that though the Church of England should listen to what other Churches have to say, to find out what they are witnessing to, it should not spend its time calculating its moves on what others will do. What matters is what is right, what is doctrine, not what is expedient.'

211. One question that does arise in this area is whether consensus requires change to proceed at the pace of the slowest mover. The Anglican-Reformed Conversations have this to say:

> Those opposed to the ordination of women argue that the force of nineteen centuries of tradition should not lightly be set aside; and that a decision on such an

issue should not have been taken by one denomination on its own, but only by a universal Council of all the Churches. All those concerned for Christian unity will take this argument seriously, so long as it is not simply a device to block all discussion and change. How long is it right to expect those in favour of the ordination of women to wait, bearing in mind that there has not been a universally recognised General Council for a thousand years? If they are truly concerned for Christian unity, both those Churches which do ordain women and those who do not will desire urgently to meet and discover one another's motives and reasons for the stand they take on this issue. (Ibid, p.64)

212. In a similar vein, Bishop Vogel of West Missouri wrote:

It is wistful, to say the least, to project an ecumenical council truly representative of Christendom in the near future. . . where General Councils cannot be called, decisions must be made beneath that conciliar level, although they should always be made on the broadest consensus possible. The ecumenical consequences of an act by a church must be seriously taken into account. . . but. . . truth — not the consequences of choosing the truth — must be the ultimate criterion in decision making. (*Pro and Con the Ordination of Women,* papers prepared for the American ARC, Seabury Press, 1976)

213. Archbishop Scott, Primate of the Anglican Church of Canada, at the time when that Church was deciding whether to ordain women, wrote:

If we are prepared to act but also to recognize that our action must be tested by experience and if we are prepared to have other churches help us to evaluate the results of the action, then we may, in fact, be making a contribution to wider ecumenical relationships. We may be helping the whole Church reflect at a deeper level. Whether our action turns out this way or not will depend in part on the attitude with which we move ahead. If we move ahead arrogantly, implying that those who disagree with our action are wrong, the action will not help ecumenical relationships. If we move ahead with conviction, but with humility and with a willingness to have the results of our action carefully evaluated, then a real contribution to ecumenical relationships may well result. (Ecumenical Review, July 1977, p.253)

VII TWO FURTHER ISSUES CONSIDERED

214. As we have seen in the last chapter, positions taken on the issue of the ordination of women are often taken because of convictions held on some quite other matter: convictions, furthermore, which have consequences over a much wider field. In this chapter, we consider two further issues that are at the very heart of the debate on women priests and where indeed much of the opposition to the ordination of women is centred, on biblical, theological and traditional grounds.

215. The first of these issues concerns the interpretation of the biblical concept of headship and the second considers the effect on concepts of priesthood and women's ordination of particular understandings of the nature of God.

Headship

216. It might be possible, on a quick reading of GS 104 Chapter IV 'The Biblical Evidence' to assume that, in the interpretation of the evidence, scholars fall into two camps: on the one hand, the conservatives and on the other, various shades of liberal opinion from the moderate to the radical. This would always have been a simplification but, in the last decade or so, evangelicals in particular are seen to cover a much wider spectrum of views. It would be simplistic to divide Anglicans into those who take the Bible seriously, and are therefore against the ordination of women, and those who are for such ordination, but pay the price of sitting lightly to the biblical evidence. What now clearly exists are strong and clear statements by evangelical scholars, all taking the Bible seriously but coming to differing conclusions on the ordination of women.

217. Dr Gordon Wenham, in an article in *Churchman* (vol. 92 No.4, 1978) The Ordination of Women: why is it so divisive?, links it directly with the role of women in the whole of life.

> The issue of ordaining women to the priesthood is much more profound and is intimately connected with the crisis of morality in our society. It is because this is dimly sensed by many, but rarely clearly articulated, that feelings run so deep and the subject can be so divisive.
>
> There are certainly those who oppose the ordination of women to leadership roles in the church on the grounds that it is incompatible with Scripture or Christian tradition. Though women could participate fully in Old and New Testament worship, and may have been allowed to pray and prophesy in charismatic churches, they were never ordained to be elders or bishops, which would have

involved them leading and teaching men. But there are many who dislike the ordination of women, though they are not really concerned that it conflicts with Scripture or tradition. Instinctively they know that men lead women and not vice versa, and they feel that the ministers ought to be model Christians. Those of a catholic outlook find it wrong to think of a woman presiding at the eucharist. This is partly because it is in this act that the priest more obviously symbolizes Christ than at any other time in his ministry, and it therefore seems right that the president should be male. But, more fundamentally still, it is at meals that in ordinary households the husband's headship comes to expression; therefore it would be wrong to have a woman administering a sacrament which takes the form of a meal. Married women and mothers tend to dislike the idea of women priests because, especially against the background of feminist ideas, it makes them feel second-class women doing less than the best for God. Previous generations of women looked on Mary, the mother of our Lord, and the women who ministered to him, as their example and inspiration. But when the church ordains women to the priesthood they see their God-given instincts of submissiveness and motherhood implicitly criticized by the church's setting up a quite different ideal of womanhood; one that owes more to the feminist movement than to Scripture, tradition or nature.

218. This strong critique of recent tendencies rests upon his understanding of the biblical evidence. He sees an obvious continuity between the Old Testament requirements for priesthood and the New Testament requirements for ministry. Though women might take a full part in Old Testament worship and might be prophetesses, they could not serve as priests, that is to say they could neither offer sacrifice nor be authoritative teachers. Of the New Testament evidence he says: 'Evidently women fully participated in the life and witness of the church, but not in its leadership.' In considering the Pauline teaching about the ministry of women, he first of all dismisses Galatians 3.28 as irrelevant since it is concerned with eligibility for baptism and not for ministry.

219. Considering whether women were allowed to participate vocally in public worship and the apparent inconsistency of I Timothy 2.12 and I Corinthians 14.33-36 with I Corinthians 11.5, Wenham is inclined to favour the view that women are allowed to pray or prophesy in church, but not to teach men. 'Praying publicly in the midst of others does not imply or involve any authority in headship over others' but Paul did not want women to occupy the position of authoritative teachers in the church.

220. Quoting 1 Timothy 2.13,14: Ephesians 5.14; I Peter 3.5, he suggests that they indicate that 'the apostles did not regard the submission of women to men as an accommodation to the ideals of their times.' He believes that this is supported by recent anthropological and biological discoveries. 'Male dominance is built into the human constitution. God created us this way.' 'The norm of relations between the sexes is that the man loves his wife, and

his wife obeys him. If women lead men this is abnormal. It upsets the God-given pattern of society.'

> Genesis 2-3 sets out the divine patterns very clearly. Man should obey God, woman obey man, and animals obey men and women. When this order is reversed, everything is blighted. Eve listened to the serpent instead of Adam; Adam listened to Eve instead of God.

He goes on to say: 'That women should obey men is only half of what Scripture has to say about marriage. . . .the other half of the picture is that every husband is expected to love his wife. . . . There should be no place for male chauvinism when Christians assert that the man should lead in marriage.' Turning to the question of church leadership, he adds:

> But once admit that the husband should lead his family, how can this role be reversed when it comes to the church? If the church is to be true to the divine realities symbolized in marriage, married women cannot be leaders of the church without destroying that symbolism. But could unmarried women be appointed to leadership roles in the church and leave the symbolism intact? I think not. In all societies unmarried women are abnormal in the sense that they are untypical; and where they aspire to leadership, they are often unfeminine as well. But a biblical ministry must reflect and embody the divine ideals for man. To give a woman teaching authority over men in the church would inevitably upset the created order.

221. It is important to recognise that for scholars such as Wenham to speak of a woman as subordinate is *not* equivalent to saying a woman is inferior. To him a subordinate is the counterpart of a leader and he believes that it is very clear that Jesus never appointed a woman as a leader (cf. the Twelve or the Seventy). Thus he does not see subordination as a result of the fall; the fall introduces male exploitation of women not the male leadership role. (These latter points are taken from a personal letter of comment).

222. Paul K. Jewett in *MAN as male and female* — A Study in Sexual Relationships from a Theological Point of View (Eerdmans 1975) sets out the relevant Pauline passages and then adds:

> We now have before us a complete summary of the New Testament passages on which the doctrine of woman's subordination is based. The woman is subject to the man because the man, as created first, is directly in the image and glory of God, whereas the woman, created after the man and for him, is the glory of the man. Because of her lesser endowment (presumably) she was deceived by the tempter when the man was not. Therefore she should never aspire to teach the man, but always learn from him in subjection and quiet humility. Specifically, this means that Christian women are not permitted to speak in church; in fact it would be shameful were they to do so. Therefore let them study a becoming silence. (*MAN as male and female,* Jewett p.61)

223. But before he comes to a consideration of the hierarchical view of the man/woman relationship, Jewett sets out the standpoint from which he starts, basing himself on Genesis 1.27. 'Man, as created in the divine image, is Man-in-fellowship; and, he adds, 'the primary form of this fellowship is that of male and female.' (Ibid, p.49). For, since God is no solitary God but the triune God (i.e. God-in-relationship), there is no possibility that man, who is in his likeness, should be solitary man.

224. Jewett notes that:

> All the Pauline texts supporting female subordination, both those that are directly from the apostle's pen and those that are indirectly so, appeal to the second creation narrative, Genesis 2:18-23, never to the first. This fact should not be overlooked, for it relates to a significant theological matter. Whereas the Bible begins its doctrine of Man with the fundamental affirmation that "God created Man in his own image, in the image of God created he him, male and female created he them" (Gen.1:27) and regards the account of the woman's creation from the rib of the man as supplementing this fundamental affirmation, Paul hardly ever refers to Genesis 1:27. (Ibid, p.119)

He therefore makes a careful analysis of the Second Creation narrative and says:

> We can only conclude, therefore, that when the narrative in Genesis 2 speaks of the woman as made from the man, the intent is to distinguish her from the animals by implying her essential likeness to the one from whom she is taken. *Her superiority over the animals, not her inferiority to the man, is the fundamental thought in the immediate context.* However, when the rabbis read in Genesis 2 that the woman was made *from* the man, they came to infer from this that she was *under* the man. But such an inference is an obvious *non sequitur;* derivation does not entail subordination. Such exposition reflects the patriarchal relationship between the sexes which was an historical fact in Israel rather than the necessary meaning of the text itself. So far as Genesis 2 is concerned, sexual hierarchy must be read into the text; it is not required by the text. (Ibid, p.126)

225. As a result of a long examination of the biblical passages Jewett says:

> We have rejected the argument for female subordination as being incompatible with (a) the biblical narratives of Man's creation, (b) the revelation which is given us in the life of Jesus, and (c) Paul's fundamental statement of Christian liberty in the Epistle to the Galatians. To put matters theologically, or perhaps we should say hermeneutically, the problem with the concept of female subordination is that it *breaks the analogy of faith.* The basic creation narratives imply the equality of male and female as a human fellowship reflecting the fellowship in the Godhead; and Jesus, as the perfect man who is truly in the image of God, taught such equality in his fellowship with women so that one may say — must say — that "in Christ there is no male and female." Any view which subordinates the woman to the man is not analogous to but incongruous with this fundamental teaching of both the Old and the New Testaments. To affirm that woman, by definition, is

subordinate to man does not correspond to the fundamental radicals of revelation; rather it breaks the analogy of faith. (Ibid, p.134)

226. Of Paul he writes:

The apostle Paul was the heir of this contrast between the old and the new. To understand his thought about the relation of the woman to the man, one must appreciate that he was both a Jew and Christian. He was a rabbi of impeccable erudition who had become an ardent disciple of Jesus Christ. And his thinking about women — their place in life generally and in the church specifically — reflects both his Jewish and his Christian experience. The traditional teaching of Judaism and the revolutionary new approach implied in the life and teaching of Jesus contributed, each in its own way, to the apostle's thinking about the relationship of the sexes. So far as he thought in terms of his Jewish background, he thought of the woman as subordinate to the man for whose sake she was created (I Cor. 11:9). But so far as he thought in terms of the new insight he had gained through the revelation of God in Christ, he thought of the woman as equal to the man in all things, the two having been made one in Christ, in whom there is neither male nor female (Gal.3:28). (Ibid, p.112)

227. It is not easy to summarise the interpretation of the Pauline passages by scholars since, inevitably, they call for long and careful exegesis, but some quotations from a *Churchman* article by Canon Colin Craston may be useful. Of the meaning of headship he says:

In relating Pauline teaching in I Corinthians to Genesis, the key issue revolves round the meaning of the word 'head'. What does Paul mean when he speaks of man as head of the woman?. . . . According to commentators on. . . .I Corinthians such as C.K. Barrett and F.F. Bruce, the word (kephale) for head denotes source, origin, not leadership, rule, direction or management. (*Churchman*, vol:92. No:4, 1978 pp.306-307)

228. C.K. Barrett, commenting on I Corinthians 11.3, says: '*Man is the head of the woman* in the sense that he is the origin, and thus the explanation of her being. That *God is the head of Christ* can be understood in a similar way.' (*The First Epistle to the Corinthians,* C.K. Barrett, Black, 1968, p.249)

229. F.F. Bruce, commenting on the same:

As for the order of creation, there is a hierarchy of the order: God-Christ-man-woman. Each of the first three members of this hierarchy is the head of the member following. By head in this context we are probably to understand not, as has frequently been suggested, "chief" or "ruler" but rather "source" or "origin". (1 and 2 Corinthians, F.F. Bruce, Oliphants, 1971, p.103)

230. Craston continues in his article by summarising the section on 'Subordination' in an article by Michael Williams (The Man/Woman

Relationship in the New Testament *Churchman*, January 1977).

In modern thought the head is regarded as the place of command, because of our view of the brain as directing the whole body. Hence, such words as 'headmaster', 'headquarters'. The Hebrew view was quite different. There is no Hebrew word for brain. The directing centre of the personality was not located in the head, but in the heart and guts. Had St Paul wished to speak of man as ruler or director of woman he would have had to use the word 'heart' — or 'lord' — to describe the relationship. This he avoids. Both Hebrew and Greek words for head are closely related to origin or source — as may be illustrated from a phrase like 'head of a river'. So St Paul speaks of man as being the origin of woman (as in Genesis 2), not her chief or ruler.

The theological factor to consider relates to the doctrines of the Trinity, creation and the church. In 1 Corinthians 11:3 St Paul deals with the headship of man in parallel with the relationship of Christ to God. When God is described as head of Christ it is not in the sense of ruling or having authority over, but as source: 'begotten of the Father before all worlds'. As Michael Williams argues, to take the passage as teaching a subordinationist view of woman commits one to a subordinationist view of Christ. From other New Testament passages it may be deduced that the headship of Christ to creation and the church again signifies source. If rule or authority over either is in view lordship is the term used, but *kurios* and *kephale* must not be taken as equivalents. (Ibid, p.307)

231. He goes on to consider headship — the fall and the new creation.

In Genesis 3:16 there is explicit reference to man's rule over woman. The context is all important. It is as a direct consequence of the Fall that subjection of woman to man, and that specifically within the marriage relationship, comes about. Subjection of woman is a dire result of sin rather than a fundamental principle of God's pattern for human life, a result all too evident in the history of man. We are not faced here with a divine provision of the creation order.

If, then — and this must be fundamental to any biblical view of sexuality in mankind — subordination of woman to man is a result of the broken relationship with God, we must expect the new creation, established through the cross, to provide the remedy. The cross has made possible the reversal of the effects of sin. On the basis of a restored, indeed a new, relationship with God the redeeming of, and new developments within, interhuman relationships become possible. And that includes the possibility of a new relationship between man and woman — Genesis 1 and 2 instead of Gensis 3. Domination on the one hand, and subordination on the other, are inconsistent with the new creation inaugurated at the cross. This is what St Paul is getting at in Galatians 3:28, surely, when he speaks of there being in Christ neither male nor female, Jew nor Gentile, bond nor free.

232. Craston refers, (as Jewett also does) to the parallel with slavery.

In respect of another human institution of his day, slavery, St Paul teaches that the inner relationship between master and slave is changed by the cross, even though both still live within the social order of the day. As the kingdom becomes more clearly and widely established, the changed inner relationship may be matched by a changed social order, as the developments of history permit principles inherent in the gospels to be applied. The formal abolition of the insitution of slavery took a long time. It has also taken a long time for the change in the man-woman relationship made possible at the cross to begin to be reflected in the social order.

233. Although arguments about the meaning of headship are important for the debate on the ordination of women, they are as much concerned with the right ordering of society according to God's will as with the ministry. This is clear from Wenham and the article by Michael Williams referred to above is more concerned with the man/woman relationship in marriage than in the ministry.

234. Within the spectrum of Evangelical understanding of headship may be found an intermediate position. This is well illustrated by Dr John Stott in his forthcoming book: *Issues Facing Christians Today* (Marshall-Pickering, 1984) in the chapter 'Women, Men and God.' He concludes his section on equality thus:

> Sexual equality, then, established by creation but perverted by the Fall, was recovered by the redemption that is in Christ. What redemption remedies is the Fall; what it recovers and re-establishes is the Creation. Thus men and women are absolutely equal in worth before God — equally created by God like God, equally justified by grace through faith, equally regenerated by the out-poured Spirit. In other words, in the new community of Jesus we are not only equally sharers of God's image, but also equally heirs of his grace in Christ (1 Pet.3.7) and equally indwelt by his Spirit. This Trinitarian equality (our common participation in Father, Son and Holy Spirit) nothing can ever destroy. Christians and Churches in different cultures have denied it; but it is an indestructible fact.

There follows a section on complementarity beginning:

> At the same time, although men and women are equal, they are not the same. Equality and identity are not to be confused. We complement one another in the distinctive qualities of our own sexuality, psychological as well as physiological, and this fact forms the basis of our different and appropriate roles in society.

235. In his final section on ministry, he considers the biblical evidence and adds:

> Whether, although the requirement of 'submission' is of permanent and universal validity, because founded in creation, the requirement of 'silence', like that of head-covering of I Corinthians 11, was a first-century cultural application of it? It is possible, then, that the demand for female silence was not an absolute prohibition of women teaching men, but rather a prohibition of any kind of teaching which infringes the principle of male headship.

He concludes that 'there are situations where it is entirely proper for women to teach, and to teach men, because, in so doing they are not usurping an improper authority over them'. But for this he says there are three conditions relating to content, context and style of preaching.

If the content is biblical, the context a team and the style humble, then surely women may teach men, since in so doing they are not claiming a headship which is not theirs. Does this mean, then, that women could and should be ordained? The difficulty I have in giving a straight answer to this question is due to the layers of muddle which have been wrapped round it. What is 'ordination'? And to what kind of 'ministry' is it the gateway? Christians of Catholic persuasion tend to say that women cannot be 'priests'. But since I do not believe the pastoral ministry to be 'priestly' in a Catholic sense, that is not my problem. Christians of Reformed persuasion tend to see the presbyterate as a fixed office which necessarily involves both authoriative teaching and the exercise of discipline, and is therefore not open to women. But it is doubtful if the New Testament gives us a rigid blueprint of ministry in which all pastors are 'teaching elders' in the Reformed mould.

Supposing the oversight envisaged in the New Testament is not priestly in the Catholic sense but pastoral; and supposing it is not necessarily presbyteral either in the fixed Reformed sense of authority and discipline, but more fluid, modest and varied, offering different kinds and degrees of ministry; and supposing ordination involves the public recognition of God-given gifts, together with the public authorisation to exercise them in a team — are 'ministry' and 'ordination' conceived in these ways to be denied to women? I cannot see why. It is true that local church pastors are described as 'over' the congregation in the Lord, and that the congregation is told 'obey your leaders and submit to their authority'. If all ordained Christian ministry inevitably has this flavour of authority and discipline about it, then indeed I think we would have to conclude that it is for men only. But if there are circumstances in which the pastoral care of people is a much more modest ministry, and the style of exercising it is humble, then no biblical principle is infringed if women are welcomed to share in it. I hope it is clear that the fundamental issue before the Church is neither 'priesthood', nor 'ordination', but the degree of authority which necessarily inheres in the presbyterate.

236. From a similar point of view, a Bishop writes:

So for me, the issue comes down to the major expression of headship — the ultimate headship in a relationship, be it of marriage or church. That is where I have to stand — and I see the ultimate headship as the Diocesan Bishop in a Diocese (so not necessarily the Suffragans, although, of course, the Suffragans share the headship role, but I think I could readily accept a woman Suffragan Bishop). In the Parish I would also see the headship of a woman Incumbent as a problem, but not if she was the head of an Order of Sisters, where the headship would be over women.

237. We have considered the arguments concerning headship largely as they are presented by those who stand in the Evangelical tradition. Nevertheless there are those in the Catholic tradition who would use similar arguments. See for example, the paper given by the Bishop of London (Rt Rev Graham

Leonard) to the Churches' Council for Covenanting in 1982 (and printed in the *Epworth Review,* January 1984).

> When I look at the biblical revelation, in particular at the early chapters of Genesis, I find there what can only be described as the principle of subordination. It is so deeply rooted in scripture that, I believe it is normative for us. (p.45)

The Ordination of Women and the Nature of God

238. In considering the question of headship, we have seen that its relevance to the subject of the ordination of women is largely concerned with what it has (or has not) to say about the way God has designed women and men to live, and to serve in ministry as part of that living. It is not, intrinsically, about the nature of God, except insofar as that which God wills for humankind may tell us about him in his own being.

239. But there are two areas of the debate which relate directly to our conception of the nature of God: Has our understanding of the Trinity anything to say about the appropriateness of women priests? Does the doctrine of the Incarnation require a male order of ministry? Does priesthood correspond to maleness in the order of creation? This also raises the whole question of masculine language and imagery related to God. As a further development in this area there is the current debate on the priest as the icon of Christ.

240. It would appear that it is in this area, more than in any other, that deep-rooted feelings are aroused on both sides of the debate. These feelings may well go far deeper than the rational element in us, but if they touch a *non-rational* element it is not to be assumed that this is to be equated with the *irrational.* We shall understand the debate better if we are able to feel something of the force of the opposing convictions and the extent to which they can be based on an understanding of God and an understanding of our own identity as man or woman and our picture of the identity of the other gender. As the Bishop of London said in his paper to the Churches' Council for Covenanting, 'when we are talking about this matter, we are considering some of the fundamental truths about our human nature and our faith. We are dealing with the deepest primaeval truths about what we are and about our relation to God' (Ibid.p.42).

OUR UNDERSTANDING OF THE TRINITY, FATHER, SON AND SPIRIT

241. Our belief in God would be different from what it is if the Trinity was described as consisting of Mother, Daughter and Spirit or if, taking refuge in terms of common gender, we described it as consisting of Parent, Offspring and Spirit simply. (*Women in the Priesthood of the Church,* E.L. Mascall, Church Union 1958, p.24, for a fuller quotation see GS 104, para.174)

242. Father Hopko, in a chapter entitled 'On the Male Character of Christian Priesthood' (*Women and the Priesthood,* ed. Thomas Hopko, St Vladimir's Seminary Press, 1983), says: 'Human nature is the created expression of the divine nature of God the Father, Son and Holy Spirit' (p.99), and, 'multipersonal, disexual, spiritual existence is a necessity if human nature is to partake of the nature of God and reflect divine existence in the order of creation. For whatever human beings may *do,* they *are,* in their inter-personal and communal being and life, made in the image and according to the likeness of God' (p.103).

243. In another chapter in the same book, Women and the Priesthood: Reflections, Hopko says:

> The divine nature is certainly sexless. And certainly all human beings, male and female, are made in the image and according to the likeness of God. Every human person is logical and spiritual — that is, each human being has, and in a sense *is,* both word (logos) and spirit. And every human person who is part of the original creation redeemed and sanctified in the Church is made to image the one God and to do his work on earth, which is, in Christ the Holy Spirit, a priestly, prophetic and kingly ministry, whatever one's sex or vocation. But in the Church, the specific ministry of being the presbyter/episcopal head of the sacramental community, which is by grace 'recreated creation' is the specific ministry of imaging the person and effecting the ministry of the Son and Word of God incarnate in human form, in his specifically 'masculine' being and activity. The sacramental priest is not the image of God or divinity in general. He is certainly not the image of the Trinity or of the Holy Spirit. He is the image of Jesus Christ, who makes known the Father in the Spirit within the life of God's Church. And this 'image' can only be actualized and effected by certain male members of the Church, who are called and equipped for this ministry. (Ibid. p.184)

244. We have seen in the previous section that Jewett also sees Man as male — female as created in the divine image of the triune God. Later in the same book (*MAN as male and female*) he says:

> If, as the theologians have taught, there is only a personal distinction in God (Trinity), not a sexual one, then the creation of Man in the divine image as male *and* female can hardly mean that Man is like God as male *rather than* female. Since God is a fellowship of persons (Father, Son, Spirit) and Man is a fellowship of persons (man and woman), therefore Man is like God as Man in fellowship with woman, not as Man in distinction from woman.
>
> Such a conclusion, which appears to be beyond dispute, requires that we construe the masculine language about God analogically not literally, when we interpret Scripture. The univocal element in the analogy is the *personal,* not the *sexual,* meaning of the language. (p.167)

(Note that Jewett capitalises Man, when he uses it generically.)

245. In a paper *'Women in the Church'*, given to the 1983 Loughborough Conference, Sister Carol CHN said this:

There has been tentative searching to find the missing feminine in the Third Person of the Trinity. This has some good basis if we look to the feminine figure of Wisdom in the O.T. Wisdom gives knowlege of the Universe. Wisdom is the source of that intuitive sense said to be a female characteristic, a spirit, be it noted, which is intelligent, holy, clear, penetrating through all things. Then in the New Testament the Holy Spirit has the maternal office of Comforter. And yet, the Holy Spirit as St Paul and the creed defines Him is the Lord. The Lord is the power from on high who also sends us out, into the outer world, in strength and confidence. . . .a paternal office. So it seems to me that the feminine is more satisfactorily to be found in each of the Persons of the Trinity. Jesus is Wisdom as well as Word of God, and there has been the recovery of the tradition of Jesus as our Mother of which Mother Julian is a clear exponent. 'Our tender Mother Jesus simply leads us to his blessed breast through his open side and there gives us a glimpse of the Godhead.' An important word there is tenderness. Let not women, nor men neither, lose their tenderness. . . .we are in danger of that in our brutalised world. For me, the Pelican causing its own breast to bleed, image of maternal sacrifice, has been a powerfully evocative symbol of Jesus.

Yet, though Jesus is our Mother in the order of sensual nature, bringing it to rebirth in God, in the making of our essential nature the First Person is both Father and Mother: 'God Almighty was our kindly Father and God all wise our kindly Mother.' Our essential nature, says Julian, is entire in each person of the Trinity. God is of course beyond all opposites or dualities of male and female. He is, says White: 'the uncreated prototype of the contraries which permeate and differentiate creation but in Him they are not contraries, but absolute unity.'

246. In her book *Faith, Feminism and the Christ* (Fortress Press, 1983) Dr Patricia Wilson-Kastner says:

The best option for feminists within a Christian context, I suggest, is offered by a trinitarian theology. . . . Negatively, one may contend that the Trinity does not have to be so gender-specific as a more rigidly monotheistic picture of God. In the Christian tradition specific persons of the Trinity, usually the Holy Spirit, have been characterised in feminine language. Father and Son/Word usually are described in and addressed by male language. Sometimes, however, the Son is also called Mother, and the Spirit is spoken of as female. Although the linguistic history of the term 'Holy Spirit' may influence this aspect of history, the nurturing role ascribed to the Spirit also bears on this old tradition. . . . The doctrine permits inclusive language in its description of the deity. (p.124)

247. We turn now from reflection on the Trinity to an area which, for some writers flows inevitably from it whether the 'masculinity' of God entails a male order of ministry in the Church.

248. A number of modern Christologists have held that there is a radical affinity between human nature and the Person of the Word. If this is so, may it not be that not only the humanity of Jesus but also the sexual mode under which he assumed it reflects a real aspect of the eternal Word. Or must we say, on the other hand, that the eternal Word transcends the particularity of his incarnate maleness *in precisely the same way* as he transcends the particularity of his incarnate first-century Palestine Jewishness. (*Whatever happened to the Human Mind?*, E.L. Mascall, SPCK, 1980, p.146.)

We are concerned here, as Rowan Williams comments, with the theological significance of the *particular,* the concrete historicity of God's speech with us in Jesus. ('Women and the Ministry: a Case for Theological Seriousness', *Feminine in the Church, SPCK, 1984)*

249. But the *'particular'* is not arbitrary, and therefore is seen as a consistent pattern. The Bishop of London in his paper says:

> The Bible does in fact use quite consistently masculine terms about God: Father, Lord, Shepherd, King. Now I certainly do not take those terms to mean that God is masculine. The fact is, however, that in speaking to us of himself God has chosen to speak to man, in these terms and not in any others. . . . It represents, I believe the fact that in terms of our relationship to God we are essentially feminine and he is masculine to us. In other words that he always has the initiative and our duty is to respond. (Ibid, p.47)

250. Later he says: 'I believe that Christ was incarnate as male because I believe psychologically, and symbolically and to a large extent biologically, the initiative is seen as male'. (Ibid, p.48)

251. Hopko in *Women and the Priesthood: Reflections* says:

In his actions in and toward the world of his creation, the one God and Father reveals himself primarily and essentially in a 'masculine' way. This is the biblical and liturgical mode of expression which cannot be altered or abandoned without changing and ultimately destroying the revelation itself. The eternal Father of the only-begotten Son becomes, through his Son and in his Holy Spirit, the Father of all human beings made in his divine image and likeness. The Father is said to be 'maternal' in his actions, more tender and loving than the most perfect human mother. Yet he is *Father,* and not *Mother.* And his only-begotten *Son* (not *Daughter)* is the bridegroom of the Church, his Spirit-filled bride — the head of his churchly body with whom he becomes 'one flesh' in the Spirit. The Son and Word of God relates to creation (made by, for and in himself) in a masculine, and not a feminine, manner. He is incarnate in human masculine form to embrace and redeem the entire creation, filling all things with all the fulness of divine life to be his beloved body and bride. This is the biblical message, whose language and symbolism have permanent theological, spiritual, mystical and liturgical significance and value. (Ibid, p.183)

252. 'The argument that the masculine character of God requires a male order of ministry in his church is focused, theologically in the doctrine of the Incarnation.' (*The Ordination of Women,* Paul K. Jewett, Eerdmans, 1980, p.30) Jewett devotes half of his book to consideration of 'The argument that the masculinity of God entails a male order of ministry in the church', and much less to arguments based on the Nature of Women or the Nature of the Ministerial Office)

253. John Saward in *Christ and his bride,* (CLA 1977) writes:

The Bishop or priest must be male because, in celebrating the Sacraments (above all, the Eucharist), the priest does not act in his own name (*in persona propria*) but in the person of Christ (*in persona Christi.*) . . . .*Persona* here denotes the part played by an actor in the Classical theatre. . . . So too "the priest takes the part of Christ, lending him his voice and gestures." For the 'actor' who plays Christ in the Sacred drama of the liturgy, more fundamental even than his spiritual and intellectual qualitites is his gender: he has to have a man's body to play the part of Christ the God — *man.* . . . .

The priest who blesses or consecrates does not do so in his own name nor as the representative of the whole community: he reproduces the Christ of the Last Supper: he is the image of Christ. . . .

It is precisely as a person with a particular gender that a priest, with the grace of the Sacrament, images Christ, is his efficacious sign. St Thomas tells as that "Sacramental signs represent what they signify by a natural resemblance", in other words, to be a Sacramental sign of Christ the High Priest a Christian priest must at least, *look like* Christ in his human appearance. (pp.9,10)

Later he says:

Now a priest is literally an icon of Christ, created not out of paint, wood or stone by an artist, but by the Holy Spirit out of male flesh, an icon given colouring and form by the contours and dimensions of a male body. . . . A woman can no more be made a bishop or priest than water can be transubstantiated into the Blood of Christ, or wine used in Baptism. (pp.11,12)

254. On the Priest as Icon, Bishop Kallistos Ware writes:

The ministerial priest, as priest, possesses no identity of his own: his priesthood exists solely in order to make Christ present. . . . The bishop or priest is therefore an imitator, image or sign of Christ the one mediator and high priest. In short, the ministerial priest is an icon. . . . There can be no question of an identification between the priest and Christ, for an icon is in no sense identical with that which it depicts . . . . An icon is not the same as a photograph. . . .this is not to be understood grossly in a literal or naturalistic sense. The priest is not an actor on the stage, 'made-up' to look like Christ. . . . It is the function of an icon to *make present* a spiritual reality that surpasses it, but of which it acts us a sign. . . . It is the purpose of the icon not to remind us of someone absent, but to *render that person present.* Christ and his saints are present as active participants in the liturgy through their icons in the church: and Christ is likewise present in the Liturgy through his icon the priest. (Man, Woman, and the Priesthood of Christ, in *Man, Woman, Priesthood, SPCK 1978, pp.80,81)*

Summing up the Orthodox understanding of Ministerial priesthood, he says:

The priest is an icon of Christ; and since the incarnate Christ became not only man but a male — since, furthermore, in the order of nature the roles of male and female are not interchangeable — it is necessary that the priest should be male. (Ibid,p.83)

The male character of the Christian priesthood forms an integral element in this pattern of revealed God-given symbolism which is not to be tampered with. Christ is the Bridegroom and the church is his Bride: How can the living icon of the Bridegroom be other than a man? (Ibid,p.84)

255. The Roman Catholic declaration on the question of Admission of Women to the Ministerial Priesthood (*Inter insigniores*), speaking of the priest acting in the name of Christ, representing Christ, says:

The supreme example of this representation is found in the altogether special form it assumes in the celebration of the Eucharist. . . .the sacrificial meal in which the people of God are associated in the sacrifice of Christ: the priest, who alone has the power to perform it then acts not only through effective power conferred on him by Christ, but in *persona Christi* taking the role of Christ to the point of being his very image, when he pronounces the words of consecration. (para.26)

256. The response to these arguments are many and varied: Professor Keifer in a chapter on 'The Priest as Another Christ' in Liturgical Prayer (*Women and Priesthood: Future Directions:* Carroll Stuhlmueller CP, the Liturgical Press Collegeville, 1978) says:

The priest represents Christ because he represents the Church. There is no moment in the eucharistic action when the priest represents Christ apart from the Church. There is no Liturgical prayer, and in particular there is no eucharist which is not the action of the church. Attention to the sacramental sign actually used in the Roman liturgy indicates the weakness of the argument against the ordination of women on the grounds that they do not have any natural "resemblance" to Christ the head and Shepherd of the church. . . .since on the level of sign the representation of Christ is grounded in representation of the church it would seem that a woman could perform the priestly role of representing Christ as well as a man. (p.110)

257. Carroll Stuhlmueller in the same symposium writes:

Just as the symbol of bread and wine is free of sexual connotations and so is able to embrace the wide family of men and women around one table, so should the symbolic representation of Christ the priest reach out to include men and women. (Ibid. p.16)

258. The Bishop of Salisbury (Rt Rev John Austin Baker), in an unpublished paper says:

If the very idea of the priest as the icon of Christ is theologically unjustified, then it probably does not matter very much whether the icon idea is pressed to emphasise the visual medium, nevertheless, it may be worthwhile pointing out that the supreme example in Christianity of a symbolically representative material object through which Christ is made personally present namely the bread and wine of the Eucharist, media which have the ulimate authority of Christ himself is usually almost defiantly *unlike* the spiritual reality which it mediates. The water and wine have absolutely no outward features in common with Christ . . . . (In the RC Church the use of white wine was specifically enjoined for the Sacrament in order to avoid superstitious notions that might arise from the likeness of red wine to blood.)

259. Professor Richard Norris considers the question of 'The Ordination of Women and the Maleness of the Christ in *Feminine in the Church*. 'Why is it that to represent Jesus is of the very essence of the ordained ministry?' he answers: 'the business of Christian ministry is the proclamation and actualization of God-with-us; and Jesus is in his own person God-with-us.' But if the redemption which Christ is, can only be represented in a male, then it must be 'not merely *as a male,* but at least partly in virtue of the fact that he is a male that Christ is, and can be God-with-us.' This christological premise assumes 'not merely that Jesus was a male, but that male, as distinct from female, character was and is a *necessary pre-conditon* of Christ's being what he is and doing what he does. . . .' 'The mere fact that Jesus was a male settles nothing. The question . . . . is that of the significance of this or that characteristic of Jesus, (significance that is to say in the salvific work of God in Christ). . . What is important *Christologically* about the humanity of Jesus is not its Jewishness, its maleness . . . but simply the fact that he was "like his brethren in every respect." The maleness of Jesus is of no *Christological* interest in patristic tradition. . . . If the argument is to hold water, it must be intending to assert . . . that the divine essence or Nature, common to the three Persons is male.' Such a proposition Norris says, would have seemed absurd to the Church Fathers for no man has yet discovered what God is in essence and nature. Therefore 'maleness is not constitutive of Jesus as the Christ . . . Christology envisages him as the representative *human being.'* The question therefore for Norris is: 'Is the relation of a female to Jesus as the Christ essentially different from the relation of a male to Jesus as the Christ?' Because women are baptised they can and do *'share the identity of Jesus as the Christ.'* In the last resort the question is: *'Whether it is the Christ of the baptismal mystery* whom the ordained person represents, or a Christ who is in fact otherwise understood and qualified. . . . To insist then that ecclesial priesthood must be male if it is to represent Christ, is to argue that ecclesial priesthood represents a different Christ from the one the other Sacraments of the Church body forth and proclaim.'

260. Gilbert Ostdiek O.F.M. in his contribution to the symposium *Women and Priesthood* entitled 'The Ordination of Women and the Force of Tradition', writes:

> The classical formula used in theological and ecclesiastical documents to describe the relationship between Christ and the ordained priest is that in ministering the priest acts *"in persona Christi."* The understanding behind this phrase is that the ministering priest represents Christ, taking his place and acting in his name, so that the effective power of the action flows from Christ and not from the priest. The priest's representation of Christ, however, goes beyond the causality and effectiveness of the action. In keeping with the classical theological dictum that sacraments cause by signifying, there is also another dimension to the relationship in the sense that the sacramental action images Christ's own action and the priest images Christ himself by a *"natural resemblance."* (p.92-93)

261. Ostdiek later comments:

> The capital theological point still remains that sacraments are the personal saving actions of Christ in a very real sense. Would it not follow then that the minister of every sacrament truly takes the place of Christ and represents him in a visible fashion within the liturgical assembly? Thus the formula *"in persona Christi"* could be applied to each case of sacramental ministry. If we then keep in mind the theological traditions which admit valid administration of baptism and marriage by women, we have already implicitly admitted that women do and can represent Christ. This also means that we can retain the representational (imaging) character of the ministerial act, and of the person of the minister, without reducing the iconic character or figurative quality of the sacramental symbol to that of an image (icon) or representation taken in a completely literal sense in all its concrete, empirical details. In other words, the maleness of Jesus and the minister would no longer be considered essential to either the act of ministry or the recipient of the sacrament of orders. (p.93)

262. Dr Rowan Williams in his article previously cited says of the effect of arguing the 'women's issue in symbolic terms':

> What if the real effect of such symbolic argument is to reinforce patterns of inequality and or to produce deep hurt and alienation? What if this makes it hard for women (real and particular women) to belong to the Church to see it as a community of liberty or reconciliation?. . . . There is at least a strong case for saying that this kind of language and symbolism stressing the centrality of Christ's masculinity makes it impossible for many people not otherwise spectacularly silly or wicked to hear the Word of God because it ignores their real and human situation.

Here we touch on an aspect of the argument concerning the masculinity of God, and, in particular, emphasis on the maleness of Christ, not so far referred to, namely that of the predominately masculine imagery and language used that accompanies it for God in the tradition. Reaction to this, especially among women varies; Wilson-Kastner writes:

Today some feminists insist that the only possible reply to Jesus' invitation is a rejection. Because explicit and implicit masculine language and imagery about God dominate in the Christian tradition, and because institutional Christianity almost since its beginning has justified the oppression of women, many feminists regard Christianity as an evil to be discarded. (Ibid.p.1)

And she cites Mary Daly and Naomi Goldenburg as those who 'articulate the fundamental position of revolutionary or counter-cultural feminists.' However other feminists and in particular those who would call themselves christian feminists take a different view. Patricia Wilson-Kastner herself has tried 'to articulate a vision of humanity, God and Christ that is both an expression of the Christian community's experience of Christ, and also explicitly responsive to feminist concerns.' (Ibid.p.8)

263. This is not, however, to underrate the problem of language and imagery. Wilson-Kastner again: 'If we understand Christ as the inclusive one who overcomes sexism, how shall we speak of the Trinity? Does not Trinitarian language itself focus on the exclusively masculine relationship the Father, Son and Holy Spirit?' (Ibid p.133)

264. Wilson Kastner herself produces a perceptive study of the Trinity and of questions of language and imagery connected with it.

265. Dr Rowan Williams turns upside down the meaning often attached to the traditional emphases on the maleness of Christ:

Jesus' maleness is important because as a *crucified* or *marginal* or *powerless* maleness it represents as dramatically as possible the 'otherness' and the judgement of God's word upon the world's patterns of dominance. . . . So with the meaning of Jesus' maleness God is not shown more woman-like than man-like by the humiliation and death of Jesus (which would then turn it into a kind of revenge fantasy) man-in-the-abstract is not judged more severely than woman-in-the-abstract. But man-as-wielder-of-power *is* judged by the God whose embodiment among us refuses that sort of authority, and in some sense may be said to have spoken in the cause of women, as he speaks for all victims, (but also in his actual practice as remembered by the Church).

266. Some final considerations: There may be many who perceive this debate as theological abstraction. They may either simply accept the maleness of the ministry on the grounds that Jesus was a man, his apostles were men and the tradition of the Church has been of a male ministry. Or they may see no logical connection between the gender of Jesus of Nazareth and the ministry today. And those of us brought up to use masculine forms for the common gender sometimes find it painful when either this English linguistic usage is pressed into the service of the masculinity of God and the maleness of the priesthood, or when we perceive the sensitivity of others, particularly younger women, to exclusive language in worship and preaching

and hear their plea for inclusive language (i.e. language that clearly *includes* women as well as men). This is not of course *directly* related to the ordination of women to priesthood — there are many who are in favour of such ordination but thoroughly opposed to any change in language and there are others who hesitate to place women in a male-oriented priesthood. Nevertheless when the opposition to the ordination of women is grounded on the masculinity of God, questions of language, imagery and symbolism cannot be ignored.

267. We conclude by a reflection on the relationship between the Church as the Body of Christ and the priest from Bishop Oliver Tomkins:

> If as we saw, the essence of priesthood is to be the ministerial representative of the church as the Body of Christ, can the total Christ be represented by less than the total humanity? If the Gospel is that "God was in Christ reconciling the world to himself", can that reconciliation be mediated within the wholeness of the Church by a priesthood which is itself less than fully human? After centuries of travail the human race faces new possibilities of fulfilment — or of annihilation. Within that awe-ful possibility, womankind is discovering fresh openings in service to humanity. Within that openness, Christian priesthood is called to be fully human if God is to be known as fully God. (*A Fully Human Priesthood,* Rt Rev Oliver Tomkins 1984).

APPENDED NOTE 2

Surveys on Attitudes

268. Mrs Nancy Nason-Clark, a Canadian, has recently completed a Ph.D. thesis at the London School of Economics on 'Clerical attitudes towards appropriate roles for women in Church and Society: an empirical investigation of Anglican, Methodist and Baptist clergy in Southern England'. She kindly made available a provisional summary of part of her study concerned with Anglican clergy, their wives and deaconesses. These were personally interviewed.

> A sixteen page questionnaire, in addition to the semi-structured interview, were developed to address the five major areas to be investigated: attitudes towards the role of women in society and in the family; lay roles offered to women in the church; attitudes toward the ordination of women to the priesthood in the Church of England; reactions to clergywomen in Methodism and the Baptist Union; and ministerial career contingencies.

Two conclusions noted are of particular interest:

> Results demonstrated that clerical respondents opposed to the ordination of women held less egalitarian attitudes towards familial and societal roles in our contemporary culture and preferred a sexual division of lay labour for tasks included in the weekly routine of church life.

269. Quotations elsewhere in this report, e.g. on headship in chapter VII, might lead us not to be surprised at this conclusion. Part at least of the constituency opposed to the ordination of women would see such a pattern as part of God's plan for men and women. The correlation may, however, be more surprising to those in other traditions who claimed in conversation with Mrs Nason-Clarke not to share such views of women in society and to be 'restrictive' only in terms of ordination. Does this offer material for dialogue? Mrs Nason-Clarke reports that she found that:

> Responses to women's ordination from Anglican clergy and clergy wives were strikingly similar. Slightly over one-third (38 per cent) of Anglican priests reported a clear opposition. . . , 24 per cent a middle view, and 38 per cent definite favour. The profile, however, from deaconesses was markedly different, with over three-quarters noting definite favour.

270. A survey by Professor Lehman, from America, of lay church members from four denominations in England, had 347 Anglican returns (87 per cent of the sample). A significant fact that emerges is that, in

considering whether or not to accept a qualified woman, the Anglican lay church member is strongly influenced by his or her perception of the clergymen's attitude, and this identification is even stronger in the Free Churches.

VIII LEGAL ASPECTS

See GS 104, Chapter XII and GS Misc 88, paras.147-149 which supplemented and corrected it.

Legal Advice concerning Women Ordained Abroad.

271. In May 1979 a Working Group set up by the Standing Committee under the Chairmanship of Professor J.D. McClean (Professor of Law at Sheffield University) and including in its membership the then Dean of the Arches (the Right Worshipful the Rev Kenneth Elphinstone) considered the question of women's ordination as it affects the law of the Church and also under the general law and, in particular, the application of the Sex Discrimination Act 1975. As to the law of the Church, the Group accepted a legal opinion of the Dean of the Arches, the Standing Counsel to the General Synod and the Legal Adviser to the General Synod to the effect that 'any woman whenever and by whomever ordained, is prohibited by the law as it stands from exercising within the Church of England any of the functions exclusively reserved to the ordained ministry'. In their opinion this was the effect of the direction in the Preface to the Ordinal that 'no man shall be accounted or taken to be a lawful Bishop, Priest or Deacon in the Church of England, or suffered to serve in any of the said Functions (i.e. of the ordained ministry), except he be called, tried, examined and admitted thereunto, according to the Form hereunto following, or hath had formerly Episcopal Consecration, or Ordination'. The lawyers went on to say that the final words have always been construed as letting in persons who have received valid episcopal ordination even though not in accordance with the Church of England Ordinal. But the essential point, was that the direction in question (to which the provision in s.6. of the Interpretation Act 1978, that in any Act, unless the contrary intention appears, words importing the masculine gender include the feminine, does not apply), by using the noun 'man' and the pronoun 'he', without 'woman' and 'she' as alternatives, necessarily implies that only a man can in any circumstances exercise 'the said Functions'.

272. The Group also dealt at length with the application of the Sex Discrimination Act 1975 and the relevant Sections of the Report (GS 415) are:

> 17 The Sex Discrimination Act 1975 makes it unlawful to discriminate against a woman on the ground of her sex in certain matters, including employment and the conferment of authorizations or qualifications affecting engagement in a particular profession. However, by section 19 of the Act the relevant provisions

are excluded where the employment or authorization is 'for the purposes of an organized religion' and where it 'is limited to one sex so as to comply with the doctrine of the religion or avoid offending the religious susceptibilities of a significant number of its followers'. The present ecclesiastical regulations of the Church of England excluding a woman priest or deacon from exercising her ministry in England are clearly within section 19 and not unlawful.

18 If it were to become possible for a woman to exercise her ministry in the Church of England that new situation might well not fall within Section 19, as such ministry would no longer be 'limited to one sex'. If a woman were appointed as assistant curate in a parish this might be regarded as 'employment' for the purposes of the Act, as 'employment' is defined to include 'employment under a contract. . . .personally to execute any work or labour'; but permission to officiate would seem not to be employment. But any licence, authorization or permission to officiate would be within the provisions dealing with authorizations or qualifications affecting engagement in a particular profession (s.13 of the Act), 'profession' including vocation.

19 The effect of this is twofold. First, it is a further reason why any change in the present regulations would have to be by Measure which would have the effect of a statute. If a Measure declared it lawful to proceed in certain ways but maintained other prohibitions on the exercise of ministry by a woman, that would be conclusive and could not be affected by any general provisions in the earlier Act of 1975.

20 Secondly, it would have to be recognized that the effect of the Measure would be to apply the exemption for organized religion to a situation not clearly covered by the previous law as set out in the 1975 Act. Technically the exemption would be enlarged. But it is not thought that this would be a major obstacle to securing Parliamentary approval for a proposed Measure, for the substantial effect of the Measure would be to reduce the area of discrimination against women.

273. Recently the Revision Committee of the Women Ordained Abroad Measure sought the advice of Chancellor Calcutt QC and his Opinion was printed as an Appendix to their Report (GS 598Y). For convenience, this is reproduced as Appendix V.

Implications of the Sex Disqualification (Removal) Act 1919

274. The May 1984 issue of *Theology* published an article by Chancellor Newsom QC. In this he argued that the Sex Disqualification (Removal) Act 1919 should apply. Section 1 is in very wide terms and is as follows:

A person shall not be disqualified by sex or marriage from the exercise of any public function, or from being appointed to or holding any civil or judicial office or post, or from entering or assuming or carrying on any civil profession or vocation, or for admission to any incorporated society (whether incorporated by

Royal Charter or otherwise) and a person shall not be exempted by sex or marriage from the liability to serve as a juror.

He went on to comment:

On the face of them, these words appear to cover a woman entering holy orders which, on any view of the matter, must be a vocation, and is usually considered also to be a profession. The only question that arises is whether the adjective 'civil', before the words 'profession or vocation' limits the effect of the Act to professions or vocations other than holy orders. The same question arises in regard to the phrase 'civil. . . .office or post'; for a benefice is certainly an office and an assistant curate holds a post.

He concludes:

Parliament is supreme and the natural meaning of the words used at least covers the 'vocation' of holy orders, which surely also is a 'profession'. It follows that it is at least strongly arguable that a woman has not been disqualified by sex (or marriage) for ordination since 23rd December 1919, and therefore that if a woman is today ordained by a bishop in accordance with the Ordinal and the ordinary rules, the secular courts would hold that she is a priest or deacon as the case may be.

He then further considered the 1975 Sex Discrimination Act.

275. A lawyer, who is a member of General Synod, in a private communication refers to the Interpretation Act 1978 Section 6 which provides that, in any Act, unless the contrary intention appears 'words imparting the masculine gender include the feminine'. The provision does not apply to Acts passed before 1850 (Schedule 2 of the 1978 Act Part 1.2) except for a criminal law provision (Schedule 2 Part 1). The Act of Uniformity 1662, which is relied upon in the legal advice in GS 415, is of course long before 1850. The Act of 1919, relied upon by Chancellor Newsom, he considers only refers to the removal of certain barriers to women: public functions, such as appointments to civil service, or judicial posts, entering civil professions and vocations, admissions as solicitors and admissions to degrees. If the Act had been intended to cover the Church of England Ministry, it would have had to make such provision.

IX HOW DOES THE CHURCH OF ENGLAND LIVE WITH THE DEBATE?

276. After twelve years — and more — of debate the Church of England is still wrestling, not just with this question but with the even larger one, 'How do we come to a decision?' In what ways can Scripture, Tradition, Reason and Experience speak to us, and, do they still leave us divided? How do we discover the *sensus fidelium*? And is it Church of England mind, an Anglican mind, or does the *sensus fidelium* demand the assent of the Universal Church? And, as we have seen, when we seem to be discussing the ordination of women, we may really be debating something quite else. For example, the Church of England seems to be living with a plurality of views on the meaning of priesthood and on the nature of biblical authority. The most urgent question may be, can we live with divergent views on this issue, and if so how?

277. There is a short chapter in GS 104 on the manner of the debate (pp.84-85) which remains as relevant as ever after twelve years. Those who have lived through these years have been increasingly conscious of the real pain and anger and fear for the future on both sides of the debate. This was vividly illustrated during a discussion of the failure of the English Covenant when anger and hurt was being expressed by those who had been in favour. A priest said: 'You must remember that the opposition is also angry: ever since the 1978 debate on the ordination of women, we feel we are being driven out of the Church of England.' Yet anyone who has had to minister after the 1978 vote to those women who feel called to priesthood, or to stand by clergy members of Synod who felt that they had somehow 'let down' these very women, cannot fail to perceive their hurt and anger. And all the time synodical process itself seems to press inexorably towards a 'win or lose' situation.

278. In the July 1984 debate on the Women Ordained Abroad Measure, the Archbishop of Canterbury said: 'I should rather like to conclude with an observation of a rather different kind — the danger of wrangling over procedures rather than facing the substantive theological issues. We ought to be talking about Scripture, Tradition, Reason and Experience, not Standing Orders.' He went on to wonder whether we were not reaping the reward of the 1975 resolution, that there were 'no fundamental objections', a form of resolution he had always regretted.

279. That resolution 'broods over', so to speak, all the later debates: for some it is no more than an opinion of Synod members, for others it is the

decisive voice of the Church of England. Perhaps the truth lies somewhere in the middle, that it has something of the character of an unratified treaty. The Church of England, when she 'declares doctrine', characteristically does so by *doing* something, usually passing a Measure, or Canon or Service by prescribed majorities and, in so doing, declaring that to be consonant with doctrine in the Church of England.

280. Meanwhile, the question remains: how and where is creative dialogue to take place? How are we to live together in our dividedness and how are we to break through the fear and the frustration? How are we to answer the question posed in GS 104, p.5: 'What will further the Gospel?'

APPENDIX I

Statement by the Archbishop of Canterbury (Dr F.D. Coggan) to General Synod 20th February 1979

THE ORDINATION OF WOMEN

The Chairman: In the course of the debate on the ordination of women on 8th November last, the Bishop of St Albans made the suggestion that it would be fruitful to initiate talks on a tripartite basis between our own Church and the Roman Catholic Church and the Orthodox Church. The Standing Committee, in giving consideration to this suggestion, asked me if I would have a preliminary informal discussion with Cardinal Hume. This I was glad to do, and the discussion took place at Lambeth Palace on Friday, 12th January. The Bishop of London was also present.

I reminded the Cardinal that the Synod had, in its debate on the ordination of women to the priesthood, been much impressed and influenced by what he had said in his address to it on 1st February, 1978. It had noted the warning he had given about deciding to ordain women unilaterally, and also his observation that in the Church of God the faith and its formulation, tradition and ministries should be decided in consultation with other local Churches. I hoped, therefore, that since the Synod had postponed a decision, he would be able in due course to give us his guidance as to how the dialogue should continue. The Cardinal gave me assurances that he would discuss the whole question with the Pope in the near future.

As to the Orthodox, I am glad to tell members of the Synod that the Bishop of St Albans, in the course of a period of sabbatical leave, is, in his capacity as Chairman of the Anglican/Orthodox Conversations, visiting the Patriarchates in Istanbul, Jerusalem, Cyprus, Athens, Alexandria, Belgrade, Sofia, Bucharest, and Moscow. During these visits he will take the opportunity of discussing the matter of the ordination of women with leaders of those Churches.

When Cardinal Hume has been able to consult with the authorities in Rome, and when the Bishop of St Albans has been able to report on his visits to the Orthodox, we shall be able to see our way forward more clearly. We must also, of course, continue to keep in touch with the Old Catholics.

It would seem to me also to be the course of wisdom, not to say of courtesy, to keep in close touch with those Churches, such as the Methodist and the Lutheran and other Churches of the Reformed tradition, which already ordain women in their ministries. It is for the Anglican Communion as such, and not for the Church of England as one part of it, to enter into dialogue with other Churches. In pursuance of the Lambeth Conference Resolution 21(5), 'promotion of dialogue concerning the ordination of women' is on the agenda for the Anglican Consultative Council which is to meet in May in London, Ontario.

The ordination of women raises theological questions of fundamental importance. We must remember that theological discussions have been proceeding for many years with other Churches, of which the ARCIC discussion is one notable example. We see its fruit in the three Agreed Statements, on Eucharist, Ministry and Authority. These reveal a sufficient consensus to give us hope that a new discussion on such matters as the place of women in the Christian life and ministry can be profitably pursued.

I would also remind the Synod that much more than theological discussion was intended. The Malta Report itself envisaged co-operation in the pastoral, social and educational fields. We do well to listen to the conclusion of the final Agreed Statement: 'Doctrinal agreements reached by theological commissions cannot, however, by themselves achieve the goal of Christian unity. . . .a unity at the level of faith which not only justifies but requires action to bring about a closer sharing between our two Communions in life, worship and mission.' This has been taken up in the FOAG report which the Synod will be debating on Thursday. I very much hope that action will be taken along these lines, both in England and elsewhere, as well as maintaining and developing relations with other Churches.

APPENDIX II

(GS Misc 85 and 85a) Versailles Consultation

To: The Primates of the Anglican Communion

I have pleasure in sending the Joint Report of the Anglican/Roman Catholic Consultation concerning the Ordination of Women. This is the Consultation referred to in "Preparatory Information" for the Lambeth Conference 1978, page 57(d). I apologise that it has not been possible to send it to you earlier.

The Anglican circulation of the Joint Report of the Consultation held last February/March is made with the knowledge of the Vatican Secretariat for Promoting Christian Unity, with whom we have been in close association throughout. In our discussions subsequent to the completion of the Report the Secretariat for Promoting Christian Unity has stressed that the Report must be read as a whole, and in particular that paragraph 6 should not be separated from paragraph 2 and 3. The Anglican understanding also is that the document be read as a single whole, in the light of the Terms of Reference given to the Consultation: "To what extent and in what ways churches with women priests and churches without women priests can be reconciled in sacramental fellowship". It will be seen that the subject of the Report is not an investigation of the grounds for or against the ordination of women to the priesthood, or of the possibility of changes of mind or practice on either side.

Each Primate is free to distribute the Report in his Province as he may wish. Several copies are enclosed; more will be available at the Lambeth Conference.

At the Lambeth Conference the Observers from the Roman Catholic Church will be able to comment on the Report. They include members from the Secretariat for Promoting Christian Unity, one of whom was also a participant in the Consultation.

Following the Resolution concerning Pan-Anglican Conversations with other Churches (ACC-2 Dublin, Report page 8) the Anglican Consultative Council at its next meeting will consider any response to the Report which you may wish to send to it.

The Report is not a restricted document, and Primates may communicate its contents as they wish.

Yours very sincerely,

signed John Howe
Secretary General
Anglican Consultative Council

The Report

1. Given that certain churches of the Anglican Communion have ordained women to the presbyterate, the question posed to the Consultation was not to discuss whether or not it is right to ordain women, but to consider 'To what extent and in what ways churches with women priests and churches without women priests can be reconciled in sacramental fellowship'

2. A substantial majority in each Anglican church accepts the possibility of ordaining women to the presbyterate. Some churches have already proceeded to such ordinations. At this time no Anglican church has officially stated that such ordinations are impossible, though some churches have not yet considered the question officially and others have for various reasons decided not to ordain women at least for the present. The Roman Catholic Church believes that she has not the right to change the tradition 'unbroken throughout the history of the Church, universal in the East and in the West', and considered to conform to God's plan for his Church.

3. Given these two positions the question must be: is it still possible for our two churches to establish full communion between them and if so how, since full communion presupposes the mutual recognition of ministry? On the one hand could the Roman Catholic Church, which judges it impossible, for theological reasons, to ordain women, recognize such ordinations in the Anglican Communion? How could she hold such ordinations impossible for her yet possible for the Anglican Communion?

4. On the other hand, many Anglicans find it difficult to accept the official Roman Catholic position (as expressed for example in the Declaration *Inter insigniores*) that the ministry of the Church is not open to this development.

Many Anglicans consider the ordination of women to be both faithful to tradition and to express a legitimate new development. Within the tension and divergence which they are experiencing over this question, the autonomous provinces of the Anglican Communion believe they are expressing their real sense of unity in diversity.

5. With the Statements of the Anglican-Roman Catholic International Commission and with the sharing and collaboration which are growing everywhere between Anglicans and Roman Catholics, we continue to discover new hopes of unity: hence it has seemed to us necessary to pose the problem in its clearest form. Because of their mututal esteem neither communion can take lightly the fact that the other seems either to do something not warranted by the will of Christ for his Church or to be lacking in sensitivity to the promptings of the Holy Spirit.

6. Two things may be seen as ground for hope. First there is the fact that those Anglican churches which have proceeded to ordain women to the presbyterate have done so in the conviction that they have not departed from the traditional understanding of aspostolic ministry (expressed for example in the Canterbury Statement of the Anglican-Roman Catholic International Commission). In the second place there is the fact that the recent Roman Catholic Declaration does not affirm explicitly that this matter is *de jure divino*. These facts would seem not to exclude the possibility of future developments.

7. These developments might well be stimulated by deeper dialogue on those noticeable differences which have been emphasized by this new obstacle — matters such as human sexuality, culture and tradition, freedom and authority, among others. Simultaneously, despite the difficulty in this issue, both Anglicans and Roman Catholics feel themselves committed to continue exploring the new shapes of ministry to which the Holy Spirit may be calling them, as well as to a new sense of unity with one another. The rapidity of change in our times, the great diversities of culture and circumstance in which the churches must minister, and the growing characteristic contribution of the Third World to theology, demand openness, flexibility and a readiness to accept and affirm differences in form and style. How this is to be achieved in fidelity to the tradition which we share is one of the challenges which face the Church in our time.

8. While we do not underrate the reality of this obstacle, we are convinced that our communions ought to maintain that deep trust in each other which has been built up over recent years. We have a grave responsibility to continue and intensify co-operation and dialogue in everything that promotes our growing together towards full unity in Christ. In this the

churches will be sustained by their confidence and hope in the Holy Spirit, who alone can bring the effort to fulfilment.

Report of a Special Meeting of the Anglican-Orthodox Joint Doctrinal Commission: July 1978 (extracts).

I INTRODUCTION

(1) On 13th - 18th July 1978 the Anglican-Orthodox Joint Doctrinal Commission held a special meeting at the Inter-Orthodox Centre of the Church of Greece, in Pendeli Monastery, Athens, where they were the guests of His Beatitude Archbishop Seraphim of Athens and all Greece.

The Orthodox members represented eleven of the Orthodox Churches and the Anglican members represented the whole Anglican Communion. Two subjects were discussed: the removal of the Filioque Clause from the text of the Creed used in the Anglican Communion, and the Ordination of Women. The second of these questions has brought our dialogue to a point of acute crisis. Because of the extreme urgency of the matter, the members of the Commission meeting at Cambridge in 1977 decided to leave aside, for the time being, the agenda planned at Moscow in 1976, so as to concentrate on this problem.

(2) The Delegates gatherd at Pendeli have prepared this present report in order that it may be brought to the attention of the forthcoming Lambeth Conference and be taken into consideration in any recommendations that it makes to the Churches of the Anglican Communion.

We note that these issues, together with the general subject of Anglican-Orthodox relations, figure on the Agenda of the Conference.

III The Orthodox Position on the Ordination of Women to the Priesthood

The Orthodox Members of the Commission unanimously affirm the following:

(1) God created mankind in his image as male and female, establishing a diversity of functions and gifts. These functions and gifts are complementary but as St Paul insists (1 Cor.12), not all are interchangeable. In the life of the Church, as in that of the Family, God has assigned certain tasks and forms of Ministry specifically to the man, and others — different. yet no less important — to the woman. There is every reason for Christians

to oppose current trends which make men and women interchangeable in their functions and roles, and thus lead to the dehumanization of life.

(2) The Orthodox Church honours a woman, the Holy Virgin Mary, the Theotokos, as the human person closest to God. In the Orthodox tradition women saints are given such titles as Megalomartys (Great Martyr) and Isapostolos (Equal to the Apostles).

Thus it is clear that in no sense does the Orthodox Church consider women to be intrinsically inferior in God's eyes. Men and women are equal but different, and we need to recognise this diversity of gifts. Both in discussion among themselves and in dialogue with other Christians, the Orthodox recognise the duty of the Church to give women more opportunities to use their specific charismata (gifts) for the benefit of the whole people of God. Among the ministries (Diakoniai) exercised by women in the Church we note the following:

(a) ministries of a diaconal and philanthropic kind, involving the pastoral care of the sick and needy, of refugees and many others, and issuing in various forms of social responsibility;

(b) ministries of prayer and intercession, of spiritual help and guidance, particularly but not exclusively in connection with the monastic communities;

(c) ministries connected with teaching and instruction, particularly in the field of the Church's missionary activity;

(d) ministries connected with the administration of the Church.

This list is not meant to be exhaustive. It indicates some of the areas where we believe that women and men are called to work together in the service of God's Kingdom, and where the many charismata of the Holy Spirit may function freely and fruitfully in the building up of the Church and society.

(3) But, while women exercise this diversity of ministries, it is not possible for them to be admitted to the priesthood. The Ordination of Women to the priesthood is an innovation, lacking any basis whatever in Holy Tradition. The Orthodox Church takes very seriously the admonition of St Paul, where the Apostle states with emphasis, repeating himself twice: 'but if we or an angel from heaven preaches to you anything else than what we have preached to you, let him be Anathema. As we have already said, so I say to you now once more: if anyone preaches to you anything else than what you have received, let him be Anathema'. (Gal.1.8-9). From the time of Christ and the Apostles onwards, the Church has ordained only men to the priesthood. Christians today are bound to remain faithful to the example of our Lord, to the testimony of Scripture, and to the constant and unvarying practice of the

Church for two thousand years. In this constant and unvarying practice we see revealed the will of God and the testimony of the Holy Spirit, and we know that the Holy Spirit does not contradict himself.

(4) Holy Tradition is not static, but living and creative tradition is received by each succeeding generation in the same way, but in its own situation, and thus it is verified and enriched by this renewed experience that people of God are continually gaining. On the basis of this renewed experience the Spirit teaches us to be always responsive to the needs of the contemporary world. The Spirit does not bring us a new revelation, but enables us to relive the truth revealed once for all in Jesus Christ, and continuously present in the Church. It is important, therefore, to distinguish between innovations and the creative continuity of tradition. We Orthodox see the Ordination of Women, not as part of this creative continuity, but as a violation of the Apostolic faith and order of the Church.

(5) The action of ordaining women to the priesthood involves not simply a canonical point of Church discipline, but the basis of the Christian faith as expressed in the Church's ministries. If the Anglicans continue to ordain women to the priesthood, this will have a decisively negative effect on the issue of the recognition of Anglican Orders. Those Orthodox Churches which have partially or provisionally recognised Anglican Orders did so on the ground that the Anglican Church has preserved the Apostolic succession, and the Apostolic succession is not merely continuity in the outward laying-on of hands, but signifies continuity in Apostolic faith and spiritual life. By ordaining women, Anglicans would sever themselves from this continuity, and so any existing acts of recognition by the Orthodox would have to be reconsidered.

(6) 'If one member of the body suffers, all the other members suffer with it' (1 Cor. 12:26). We Orthodox cannot regard the Anglican proposals to ordain women as a purely internal matter, in which the Orthodox are not concerned. In the name of our common Lord and Saviour Jesus Christ, we entreat our Anglican brothers not to proceed further with this action which is already dividing the Anglican Communion, and which will constitute a disastrous reverse for all our hopes of unity between Anglicanism and Orthodoxy. It is obvious that, if the dialogue continues, its character would be drastically changed.

IV Anglican Positions on the Ordination of Women to the Priesthood

1. The Anglican members of the Commission are unanimous in their desire to accept and maintain the tradition of the Gospel, to which the Prophets and Apostles bear witness, and to be true to it in the life of the Church. They

are divided over the ways in which that tradition should respond to the pressures of the world, over the extent to which the tradition may develop and change, and over the criteria by which to determine what developments within it are legitimate and appropriate. In the case of the Ordination of Women differences have become particularly acute and divisive within our Communion now that the convictions of those in favour of it have been translated into action in certain national Churches.

2. On this question there is a diversity of views, which was reflected in the two Anglican papers circulated for discussion by the Commission. There are those who believe that the Ordination of Women to the Priesthood and the Episcopate is in no way consonant with a true understanding of the Church's catholicity and apostolicity, but rather constitutes a grave deformation of the Church's traditional faith and order. They therefore hope that under the guidance of the Holy Spirit, this practice will come to cease in our Churches. There are others who believe that the actions already taken constitute a proper extension and development of the Church's traditional ministry, and a necessary and prophetic response to the changing circumstances in which some Churches are placed. They hope that in due time, under the guidance of the Spirit, these actions will be universally accepted. There are others who regret the way in which the present action has been taken and believe that the time was not opportune nor the method appropriate for such action, although they see no absolute objection to it. Some of them hope that through the present situation a way forward may be found which will allow for the distinct and complementary contributions of men and women to the Church's ordained ministry.

3. The present crisis in our conversations with the Orthodox has forced all of us to reconsider the way in which, in our Communion, decisions are made on matters of such fundamental importance. How far in such questions should consensus precede action? How far may the experience of such actions itself lead to a new consensus? What methods of decision and debate are appropriate in such matters? Should the Synods of particular church provinces have the freedom to make decisions in matters which affect not only the whole Anglican Communion, but also our relations with all other Churches? Is the traditional Anglican claim to have no specifically Anglican Scriptures, Creeds, Sacraments and Ministry, but only those of the Universal Church, put in jeopardy by actions of this kind? What is the ecclesiological significance of the fact that we now have a Ministry not universally recognised within our own Communion? Where does our authority in such matters lie? We do not prejudge the answers to these questions but we believe that it is vital that they should be faced and answered.

4. In our discussions at this conference we have found a real willingness to listen to one another, to respect one another's view-points and to hear what those we disagree with are saying. This has brought the discussion on this subject to a welcome level of serious theological exchange which has helped us to find a common language of discourse. It has also given us a new hope that God will show us a way through our present divisions. We believe it to be part of our responsibility to the Gospel, and of our obedience to our Lord Jesus Christ, the only Lord of the Church, to continue together in dialogue with one another, as well as with all our Christian Brethren who are willing to enter into conversation with us. We are grateful to our Orthodox Brethren for their contribution to our reflections on this matter, and we look forward to the continuance of our conversations with them. There is no doubt in our minds that there are still large areas to be explored concerning the place of men and women in the ministry (Diakonia) of the Christian Church and its mission to the world.

V Looking to the Future

We value our dialogue together and we are encouraged that our Churches and their leaders as well as the members of our Commission hope that it may continue under conditions acceptable to both sides. For in spite of all the difficulties of our dialogue, we welcome the opportunities that it provides for us to listen to and learn from each other.

APPENDIX IV

Extracts from *Women in Training:* A Report of a Working Party set up by women staff members of theological colleges and courses, (ACCM Occasional Paper No. 14, 1983)

LEARNING FROM THE MISSIONARY MOVEMENT

18. As we have already indicated it is impossible to give a comprehensive view of women in the history of the Church. All we can do is to point to some important areas which can be quarried and built upon. From the middle of the last century it is fascinating to plot the rise and development of the missionary movements and to see the role women played in the mission of the Church. By the mid-1890s in Britain there were at least four different patterns of women's work to be observed within the 'home' churches: the voluntary women engaged in pastoral and philanthropic visiting; the bible women and deaconesses of Nonconformity and Pennefather; the newly established orders; and the deaconesses of institutional Anglicanism. At the same time overseas missionary work remained largely a male preserve. It was conceded that wives would go abroad with their missionary husbands and a few single women, often widows and daughters of missionaries, might be

engaged to look after missionary children or to teach. There were also small numbers of women missionaries engaged in zenana educational work in India. But in normal recruiting the traditional denominational societies turned women away. A woman's place was in the home and in any case women sent abroad were likely to get married with an unbecoming and wasteful haste. Moreover, the preaching of the gospel in any formal manner was in the main a clerical responsibility. The only likely role for a woman was supportive and philanthropic, for example in the teaching or medical professions.

19. Yet, despite this, by the end of the century societies such as the Church Missionary Society, the China Inland Mission, the London Missionary Society and the Wesleyan Methodist Missionary Society were all employing women, and often on a fairly large scale. For example, up until 1887 the CMS did not formally recruit women — at most 9 per cent of its missionaries in the 1870s were women — but between 1891 and 1900, 388 women, or 56.46 per cent of its total intake, were women. The reasons for the change are to some extent debatable and uncertain, but there is no doubt that Nonconformity, the revivalist and holiness traditions and the development of women's work 'at home' on the religious front, and the pressures of society together with the determination of women themselves on the secular front influenced CMS. After all, Hudson Taylor of the CIM, as early as 1868, had argued in favour of single women missionaries on the grounds that they would only be doing what was already accepted for women in church activities at home. And in 1895 he was to write in a letter to his son: "I think that women may do what God has given them the gift for, if they do it in a womanly way, and that what Paul wanted was order in the church and not talking, also that the husband should be the head". Taylor was a pioneer. In the first party of eighteen missionaries who sailed under the banner of CIM in the *Lammermuir* in 1865 there were nine single women, two wives and seven men. In one of the last which converged on West China in 1949 there were thirty-eight women and only eleven men, ready for "all manner of service", especially church building and church planting. Today, the Overseas Missionary Fellowship (CIM's successor) keeps up the tradition: 60 per cent of its missionaries in 1977 were women.

20. When we examine the roles of these women we can only come to the conclusion that there is no ministry of the church which women missionaries have not in effect carried out. They have planted, nurtured, overseen and pastored churches; they have been translators, teachers, doctors, nurses, and community workers. Yet, depending on mission, tradition or culture, there have nearly always been areas of responsibility from which they have been debarred. In some instances women did not conduct baptisms or officiate at weddings, male missionaries always being invited in for such special

occasions; but they did preside at communion services and take funerals where necessary! In other instances the opposite held. One member of the group records, "My own experience of missionaries and their roles over a period of eight years in East Africa confirmed this ambiguity of practice. The most saddening aspect of such ambiguity which came to my notice was the willingness of Anglican societies to let women plant churches and build them up (perhaps over a period of twenty to thirty years) only to require them to hand them over to ordained men (mostly young and new from the 'home' church) for pastoring. Only leadership roles seemed to be denied women, at least in theory. This is evidenced in evangelical missions by the refusal to women of roles associated with ordination and the exclusion of women from boards, councils and administrative posts".

21. The missionary expansion of the church owes an immense amount to women, much more than it is ready to acknowledge at present. Moreover, the roles these women have fulfilled have been as varied as those of their male colleagues. It is not so much that there are distinctly 'female' and 'male' roles within the church but that God gives to some men and some women special gifts to carry out particular tasks. An understanding of the part played by women and indeed by women and men together in the missionary expansion of the church would form an exacting component of theological education and have much to say about our understanding of the church's ministry when women are encouraged to play a leading part. Women in training would surely find inspiration in the lives and witness of these pioneers.

TWENTIETH CENTURY DEVELOPMENTS

22. Clearly for most women in training the more recent developments in the century will be important for setting the context for their own entry into the professional ministry of the Church, and yet we believe little attention is given to such recent developments in any of our college courses.

23. If we look at the pattern of women's accredited ministry in the first half of this century we can see that it was a fairly rigid one, almost entirely parochial and confined to inner city areas. Posts were normally defined in terms of the leadership of organisations, teaching and visiting, work which was almost exclusively done amongst women and children. Women had no liturgical role, except occasionally at specially arranged services for these groups. The fact that it could not be assumed that a woman staff member would even be invited to attend staff meetings was not really surprising in the context of a widely held view of ministry seen only in terms of Holy Orders. Where women showed themselves to be effective workers, however, they were increasingly accepted by the clergy as colleagues. But the burden was always upon the women to 'prove' themselves and gain recognition from the clergy.

24. All of this applied to both lay parish workers and deaconesses, but there were subtle distinctions between the two, stemming from their nineteenth century origins. The establishment of the deaconess order had been on the clear assumption that this was a revival of an early order of ministry. The deaconess was seen to hold a position within the tradition of the Church. The nineteenth century model was at pains to be seen working alongside the clergy and rejected the pattern of the autonomous lay communities of the continental deaconess orders. Deaconess ordination was seen to involve a life commitment and although celibacy was never officially binding, many deaconesses assumed it to be so. Some seemed almost to regard themselves as quasi-religious.

25. All of this tended to establish a "second class" image for parish workers which lingered on to such an extent that when the Council for the Order of Deaconesses and the Central Council for Women's Church Work united in the fifties, it became necessary to refute this idea by public statement. Nevertheless it survived until recently in a different form, in that deaconess candidates were obliged to serve as layworkers for two years and be re-selected prior to ordination. The "second class" feeling was overcome in part by some parish workers having very positive reasons for remaining as such. As all women's ministry was seen gradually in a more professional light, a lay stance could be adopted, no less professional than the deaconess, but providing the opportunity for a more exploratory or 'fringe' type ministry within the Church. Other layworkers could not see the point of becoming deaconesses and there was some resistance to the public commending of the deaconess order by some bishops.

26. The second half of the present century saw changes being taken further and some of the less satisfactory role models abandoned. This has been due to changes in the position of women in society, even though the Church has tended to be slow in reflecting these. Women are seen less as assistants to the clergy and more as having a ministry in their own right for which they bear responsibility. In ministry these women are seen less as lay leaders and more as enablers and facilitators. This involves them in counselling, teaching and recruiting, generally equipping others to play their part in a missionary church. They share a general pastoral responsibility with other members, often having care of an area of a parish. Job descriptions tend to be couched less in terms of specific pieces of work and more in terms of an indication of a number of opportunities for development, making possible an initiating role as well as that of conserving and sustaining. It would appear however that a prophetic and challenging role is still not easy for most women. A role demanding a degree of aggression is not easy for those who perhaps still feel that they face a problem of acceptance. The woman who risks the unpopularity of the prophet may well find herself effectively deprived of

such ministry as she has, being seen as a "difficult woman". Thus women still have some way to go before being able to use all their gifts within the available Church structures.

27. A few are now called upon to exercise a role as a 'focus' person for the local Church community as ministers in charge of parishes or worship centres, or as quasi-team vicars. There is no way they can do this at present without the services of a priest, and this is more easily and appropriately available within a team ministry. Congregations can feel "palmed off" with a woman minister in place of a vicar. Much depends on how well they have been prepared for such a change. They may turn instinctively to a local NSM priest rather than to a full-time woman minister even though the responsibility is hers. The placing of women in new ventures may have a better chance of success than in established parishes where pastoral reorganisation is resented. Even so, there are notable exceptions to this tendency and there seems no reason to think that a woman cannot act as such a focus. There are signs of hope for the future in the number who do so effectively in interregnums.

28. As the patterns for ministry are changing more women are reflecting upon their experience and writing about their ministry. One of the most interesting chapters in the book "The Ordination of Women in an Ecumenical Perspective" is by a woman who describes what it was like for her to enter into the space hitherto filled only by men and how she had to learn to use that space, to be in it and to learn to move in it, in quite different ways from men. The recent success of Margaret Cundiff's book 'Called to be Me', and the book by Elizabeth Canham on her path to priesthood should provide illustrative material for women in training helping to counter the models of men in ministry which are most readily available.

29. This has been necessarily a selective presentation of the past, determined by the limitations of time and the lack of expertise. It does however suggest to us that women in training should be helped to see that work in the context of a lengthy history of women's involvement in the ministry of the Church. There is much to be learnt about the way women's role has been conditioned by the prevailing philosophy and theology of the ages. Women have, much less than men, been able to discover their contribution to ministry and offer it freely. But, if we let the almost silent tradition speak, there is much encouragement and many insights on which to build for the future.

30. Too often in the past the models chosen for women have been one sided or distorted, intended to encourage and foster growth in one direction. They have been roles that were supporting, retiring, nurturing and secondary to and dependent upon men, suggesting submissiveness and passivity. Mary,

for example, has been intepreted and used to reinforce submission and to value above all the role of wife and mother. We find Mother Julian and Mother Teresa, two important models today, strangely ambiguous. While not wanting to deny the deep spiritual insights of the one and the self-giving in care of the poor of the other, it is striking that their motherhood does not include the full use of their sexuality in bearing and nurturing children and the fact that celibacy is the way of both is a factor we find hard to assess. There is need to discover other powerful models for women that neither exalt the virtue of wife and mother above all else, nor appear to commend celibacy; role models which allow for greater diversity. Women's ministry needs to be seen in continuity with the diversity of the past as well as the new patterns of men's ministry, which are so often connected with power, authority, domination, remoteness and omni-competence.

31. Whilst we are certain of the need to retain the past, to write church history giving more space to the perspective of women, to their stories and experiences, we do not see this primarily as an attempt to reclaim the saints and mystics of the past from male hagiography and male domination. Rather we see it as an attempt to emphasise a silent part of our Christian story and thus to discover new and creative dimensions in the past which will point us to more completeness and wholeness.

32. This is because we believe that at the heart of the Christian faith is 'relationship'. The faith is Trinitarian, which is to say that our God is comprehended in terms of a dynamic relationship, three persons in one 'dynamos' — energy — of relating. This divine mutuality of relationship extends itself to creation where it is reflected. The principle of relating is inherent in the very nature of creation. Relationship implies complementarity: indeed it is contingent upon it. Complementarity must not be understood as negative, an expression of inadequacy on the one part, to be remedied by surplus on the other. Rather it is a positive, the good of the one being fulfilled by the new dimension created by the good of the other. Theologically speaking, the principle of complementarity is a means of providing union, of making for oneness of that which is in relation but diverse.

33. We have to consider how far complementarity is of the essence in the pressing forward with and developing of women's role in ministry. This is a complex area all too often over-simplified by asserting complementarity of function, thus limiting certain functions to women and certain others, usually priesthood, to men. History and present experience seem to suggest that complementarity of function is not the key to true complementarity.

34. Equally it is impossible to deny the initial role of gender in

complementarity. The quasi-erotic symoblism and experience of religious language points in that direction. Without the sex-specific contribution of women and men to religious transactions there would have been less mysticism, less depth in exploration of the interior implications of salvation. Nevertheless we would not want to say either on our reading of the past or of our present experience that complementarity which tends to wholeness in life and in ministry is to do with acknowledging the equality of women and men and then striving for equal participation of both sexes in ministry.

35. Complementarity is indeed to do with the relationship of opposites, but the prime category here is as much to do with the qualities of masculinity and femininity as these have come to be described by biologists and psychologists as with male and female. It is important, though very difficult to move away from the assumption that the so-called masculine characteristics are to be found in men and the so-called feminine characteristics found in women and if only we have a ministry in which men and women were complementary then this would make for wholeness and unity. In our understanding it is much more complex and delicate than this. Masculinity and femininity are perhaps even more significant than maleness and femaleness. A ministry which is whole must seek to mirror and to release in others the complementary qualities of masculinity and femininity: and seek to release and bring them into harmony both within individuals and in the community.

36. Consequently role models for women and men must be diverse and not simply be confined to female models that uphold the 'so-called' feminine characteristics and male models that uphold the 'so-called' masculine qualities. As women enter in greater numbers the set apart ministry models must bc found which do not suggest that the set apart ministry can only be fulfilled on the basis of the past male and largely masculine patterns. Wholeness in ministry means a deeper and richer complementarity, which understands difference, polarity and creative tension between male and female, masculine and feminine. Sensitivity and a willingness to be open to new patterns will lead us towards a ministry which is the paradigm of and way towards the depths of unity.

CONCLUSION

37. As we have reflected on the history of the Church in order to discover role models and clues for women in ministry today, there has been in our minds the question of whether it is to the pattern and model of hierarchicial paternalistic ordered ministry formed by men in the past 2,000 years that women are now being called. Is it not rather that women are being asked to discover new styles and patterns of ministry and priesthood, building on some of those models already there in the past? Women are surely called to

release into the Church's ministry those qualities and insights often associated with the 'feminine' which have been suppressed and stifled, thereby impoverishing the whole community. The training of women should be in part concerned with helping women to discover ways of complementing and signalling values in ministry other than those of the hierarchicial and paternalistic patterns of the past. Women need to be encouraged to discover their contribution rather than being conformed to the mould of male patterns and masculine values. One of the ways in which this might be fostered is if women, and indeed women and men together, are led in an exploration of women's roles in the past and shown the forces which conditioned those roles.

39. To search for role models to be used in training is one way of affirming that women may have a different, distinctive but complementary ministry to contribute which in its turn would affect the structures and workings of the Church. But there are other important questions which need to be raised also in relation to the training of women that were outside our brief and yet which we regard as essential. There is a growing body of feminist theology, or rather, feminist theologies, which deserve to be taken account of. They spring from the conviction of women that when women are brought into the community that reads and interprets Scripture and Tradition new things are seen in the Tradition about the nature of God, the Church and its ministry. How many College courses are responding to these challenges? Only if we are open to this and take seriously the need to draw out the contribution women can make shall we discover structures of ministry that bear witness to women and men created and redeemed in the image of God, and new and holistic ministry which can point to a way of partnership and sharing for the people of God.

APPENDIX V

Appendix to Report of the Revision Committee *Draft Women Ordained Abroad Measure* GS 598Y

An Opinion of the Worshipful David Calcutt Q.C., Chancellor of the Dioceses of Bristol, Europe and Exeter

I. *U.K. Legislation*

The relevant legislation in this instance is contained in the Sex Discrimination Act 1975, which gives rise to the following questions.

1. Is there discrimination within section 1 of the 1975 Act as a result of the Draft Measure?

    (a) So far as material, section 1 provides that:
    "(1) A person discriminates against a woman in any circumstances relevant for the purposes of any provision of this Act if —
    (a) on the ground of her sex he treats her less favourably than he treats or would treat a man. . . ."

    (b) According to section 5(3), "a comparison of the cases of persons of different sex or marital status under section 1(1). . . .must be such that the relevant circumstances in the one case are the same, or not materially different, in the other." In other words, like cases must be compared with like in deciding whether there is discrimination or not.

    (c) As regards women ordained abroad as deaconesses, no problem of sex discrimination seems to arise. Since the order of deaconesses, not being one of Holy Orders, is not equivalent to the order of deacons, no relevant comparison can be made as required by section 5(3).

    (d) Men ordained abroad as priests may be granted permission to minister in England for an unlimited period of time — Overseas and Other Clergy (Ministry and Ordination) Measure 1967 clause 1. The effect of the Draft Measure, however, is that women ordained abroad may only be authorised to minister for a period not exceeding six months in any one year. This would therefore appear to be discrimination on the grounds of sex which falls within section 1(1) of the Act.

    (e) It could also be said that there is indirect discrimination against women inasmuch as women must have been ordained abroad before they can apply to minister in England. However, since women could not previously officiate in England as priests at all, the effect of the Draft Measure would be to lessen a pre-existing discrimination rather than to impose or increase it.

    (f) Furthermore, it can be argued that any such discrimination is not on the grounds of sex but on the grounds of religious susceptibilities and therefore not within the ambit of section 1(1) at all. A case decided on totally different facts but which would perhaps be used as an analogy is *Noble* v. *David Gold & Son (Holdings) Ltd,* (1980) I.R.L.R.252 where certain women warehouse workers were made redundant in preference to men. The women claimed that there had been sex discrimination. On the evidence it was established that the women had been employed in light work and the men on heavy work and that it was the light work which was diminishing. The court held that the employer was not entitled to assume that all women were incapable of heavy work, and that he could not therefore select women for redundancy merely because they were female. However, it also held that the complainants were all in fact incapable of heavy work and that the discrimination had been on the grounds of physique and strength, not of sex.

(g) Even more cogent, perhaps, is the argument that any such discrimination is not based on sex but on the particular Church concerned. The Church of England does not permit the ordination or women whereas other Churches in communion with the Church of England do allow this. Permitting priests ordained abroad to minister in England necessarily means permitting any women priests of those Churches to do likewise. Since by reason of its doctrines the Church of England has no female priests, any discrimination against women by requiring them to be ordained abroad has no connection with their sex but only with the doctrines of the individual Churches concerned.

(h) In my view, therefore, there is a good argument for saying that the only discrimination effected by the Draft Measure on the grounds of sex is that outlined in paragraph (d) above — namely that women ordained abroad may be permitted to officiate in England for up to six months in a year only, whereas men ordained abroad are subject to no such restrictions.

2. If there is discrimination within section 1(1), is it rendered unlawful by the subsequent provisions of the 1975 Act?

(a) The relevant provision here is section 13, which so far as material provides:

"13(1) It is unlawful for an authority or body which can confer an authorisation or qualification which is needed for or facilitates, engagement in a particular profession or trade to discriminate against a woman —

(e) In the terms on which it is prepared to confer on her that authorisation or qualification. . . .''

(b) *Prima facie,* the fact that authorisation to minister may only be granted to women ordained abroad for up to six months is discrimination in the terms on which such authorisation is granted.

(c) However, it is also true that the effect of the Draft Measure is to make lawful that which was not previously lawful. Thus it can at least be argued that there is no room for any discrimination as regards the *terms* of the permission granted — either it is granted for up to six months or not at all, and no variations are possible. If the discrimination is viewed this way, then it has nothing to do with the terms on which permission is granted and section 13 cannot apply to make it unlawful discrimination. (As far as applications for six months or less are concerned no question of discrimination arises since the position of women under the Draft Measure appears to be the same as that of men under the 1967 Measure referred to above).

(d) If, on the other hand, there is unlawful discrimination, then section 19 of the Act must also be considered.

"19(1) Nothing in this Part applies to employment for the purposes of an organised religion where the employment is limited to one sex so as to comply with the doctrines of the religion or avoid offending the religious susceptibilities of a significant number of its followers.

(2) Nothing in section 13 applies to an authorisation or qualification (as defined in that section) for purposes of an organised religion where the authorisation or qualification is limited to one sex so as to comply with the doctrines of the religion or avoid offending the religious susceptibilities of a significant number of its followers."

(e) Professor McClean has argued that if women are once permitted to minister in England at all, then the protection of section 19 is lost altogether and I am inclined to think that he is right on this since there ceases to be a limitation to one sex only. Whilst the complete exclusion of women from ordination in the Church of England may still be justified within section 19(2) on the grounds of compliance with the doctrines of the religion, it seems to me that once priests of other Churches in communion with the Church of England are permitted to minister in this country, then the circumstances in which they are allowed to do so should not differ according to whether they are male or female.

(f) No problem arises of course in respect of periods up to six months since both men and women ordained abroad can be granted permission for this length of time. The difficulties occur in respect of periods exceeding six months. No doubt an argument could be constructed to the effect that permissions granted for more than six months were still "limited to one sex so as to comply with the doctrines of the religion or to avoid offending the religious susceptibilities of a significant number of its followers" — in this case communicants of the Church of England who are unused to female priests. I do not, however, feel that such an argument is tenable, especially since it would seem on the authority of *Garland* v *British Rail Engineering Ltd,* (1982) 2 W.L.R.918 that an exemption such as is contained in section 19 should be construed strictly in conformity with E.E.C. law as far as possible. In that case, it was held that the blanket exemption laid down by section 6(3) contravened E.E.C. law by virtue of its generality since it was capable of covering situations where sex was not in fact an important factor. The exemption in section 19, on the other hand, is far from being a blanket exemption as it is limited to the very narrow area of religions where sex is in fact of doctrinal significance. For this reason, section 19 in itself does not appear to contravene E.E.C. law. However, a technical construction such as that suggested above does seem to be precluded by the *Garland* case which requires such exemptions to be interpreted strictly.

(g) Even if the protection of section 19 is lost for this purpose, I accept Professor McClean's point that the Draft Measure is a liberalising measure rather than a restrictive one, clearly defining the ambit of newly lawful action, and that its specific provisions will override the general provisions of the 1975 Act according to the normal principles of Parliamentary Sovereignty and statutory interpretation. Thus even though not expressly included in section 51 of the Act (which broadly provides that no acts shall be rendered unalwful by the Act if done in accordance with prior statutory authority), I am of the opinion that a permission granted in accordance with the Draft Measure would not be struck down by the Sex Discrimination Act.

3. In conclusion, therefore, my view is that the Draft Measure does not fall foul of the 1975 Act.

(a) The continued exclusion of women not ordained abroad is probably not discrimination on the grounds of sex and even if it was, it would be justified under section 19.

(b) The six-month restriction placed on permissions granted to women ordained abroad, although it amounts to discrimination, is arguably not related to the "terms" on which such permissions are granted and therefore not rendered unalwful by section 19. Whilst probably not protected by section 19 either, the specific provisions of the Measure would in any event override the more general provisions of the Act and any permission granted under it would thus be lawful.

II *E.E.C. Law*

We are concerned here with the Council Directive 76/20/EEC of 9th February 1976 which implements the so-called "principle of equal treatment." There is no authority of the European Court of Justice itself as to whether this Directive is directly applicable so as to confer a cause of action on an individual — see *Worringham* v *Lloyds Bank Ltd,* (1981) I.C.R.558; *Burton* v *British Railways Board,* (1982) I.R.L.R.116; *Garland* v *British Rail Engineering Ltd,* (1982) 2 W.L.R.918. The only United Kingdom authority on the point suggests that it is not directly applicable and accordingly does not ground any cause of action between individuals but only as against the United Kingdom Government — see *Southampton and South West Hampshire Health Authority (Teaching)* v *Marshall* (1983) I.R.L.R.237; *Roberts* v *Tate & Lyle Food and Distribution Ltd,* (1982) I.C.R.521.

1. Does the Directive apply at all to questions of ordination and licensing/permitting to officiate?

(a) Not surprisingly, there is no direct authority on this point. Article 1 provides as follows:

"1(1) The purpose of this Directive is to put into effect in the Member States the principle of equal treatment for men and women as regards access to employment, including promotion, and to vocational training and as regards working conditions and, on the conditions referred to in paragraph 2, social security.

117

This principle is hereinafter referred to as 'the principle of equal treatment'."

(b) *Prima facie,* therefore the Directive is concerned with employment, vocational training and working conditions, none of which seem particularly apt to cover the issues raised by the Draft Measure.

(c) In view of the virtual complete absence of women priests in the Community generally and the lack of any specific religious exemption equivalent to section 19 of the Sex Discrimination Act 1975, there must surely be a strong argument that questions concerning the priesthood do not fall within the scope of the Directive at all.

2. On the assumption that the Draft Measure is nonetheless within the scope of the Directive, what is the effect of Article 2?

(a) As far as relevant, Article 2 provides as follows:

"2(1) For the purposes of the following provisions, the principle of equal treatment shall mean that there shall be no discrimination whatsoever on grounds of sex either directly or indirectly by reference in particular to marital or family status.

(2) This Directive shall be without prejudice to the right of Member States to exclude from its field of application those occupational activities and, where appropriate, the training leading thereto, for which, by reason of their nature or the context in which they are carried out, the sex of the worker constitutes a determining factor.

(4) This Directive shall be without prejudice to measures to promote equal opportunity for men and women, in particular by removing existing inequalities which affect women's opportunities in the areas referred to in Article 1(1)."

(b) I agree with Professor McClean that the priesthood is almost certain to be treated as an occupational activity where the sex of the worker constitutes a determining factor. Matters relating thereto would therefore be excluded altogether from the application of the Directive subject to Article 9(2) which provides that:

"Member States shall periodically assess the occupational activities referred to in Article 2(2) in order to decide, in the light of social developments, whether there is justification for maintaining the exclusions concerned. They shall notify the Commission of the results of this assessment."

(c) As long, therefore, as matters relating to the ministry of female priests were kept under review, there would be no breach of the Directive.

(d) I also agree with Professor McClean's analysis of the case of *Commission of the European Community* v *United Kingdom of Great Britain and Northern Ireland,* now reported at (1984) I.R.L.R.29, concerning male midwives. The decision of the European Court of Justice recognised the fact that men were not traditionally employed as midwives and that midwifery was a sphere in which respect for a patient's sensitivities was of particular importance. By analogy, the same could equally be said of religions into which women cannot traditionally be ordained and where religious sensitivities are just as important.

(e) The decision also rejected the argument that once males were permitted at all to act as midwives, then it should automatically be on exactly the same basis as women. As long as the position was kept under review as required by Article 9(2), the European Court held that the United Kingdom was in compliance with its obligations under the Directive.

(f) If any event, as I have sought to argue in I.1.(g) above, the continued exclusion from ministering in England of women not ordained abroad is not necessarily discrimination on the grounds of sex.

(g) As to the six-month restriction imposed on women ordained abroad, however, it would seem that this can be justified under Article 2(4) above since the Draft Measure will in fact liberalise their position rather than restricting it.

(h) In these circumstances, and bearing in mind the doubts as to whether the Directive is applicable at all to this situation, I am of the view that the proposed Measure does not contravene E.E.C. Law.

3. Priests ordained abroad who wish to retire to England and exercise a ministry there.

(a) If questions relating to the priesthood do not fall within the purview of the Directive, then obviously no problem arises in the context of E.E.C. Law, even if female priests would not be permitted to retire to England and minister there.

(b) If the Directive does apply, then I would have thought that Article 2(2) applies equally to that situation (subject to Article 9(2)) although there is apparent direct discrimination.

(c) I notice from paragraph 23 of the Minutes of the Revision Committee held on 18th January 1984, that retired male priests ordained abroad can apply for permission to minister under the Overseas and Other Clergy (Ministry and Ordination) Measure 1967. If the Draft Measure concerning women is adopted, I fail to see how retired women priests ordained abroad but of English nationality are precluded from applying under it for permission in a similar fashion. Any permission granted would, however, be limited to a six-month period which might anyway be justified under Article 2(4) as suggested above.

BIBLIOGRAPHY

Short bibliographies are to be found in GS 104 and GS Misc 88. Reports and books listed there are not included here unless they are referred to in this report.

Anglican Reports

GS 104. *The Ordination of Women to the Priesthood.* A consultative Document presented by the Advisory Council for the Church's Ministry (CIO, London, 1972)

GS Misc 88. *The Ordination of Women.* A Supplement to the Consultative Document GS 104. Prepared at the request of the Standing Committee by Miss Christian Howard. (CIO, London, 1978)

ACC 4 — Report, 1979 (ACC, London 1979)

ACC 5 — Report, 1981 (ACC, London 1981)

ACC 6 — Report, 1984 (CIO Publishing, London 1984)

Report of the Lambeth Conference, 1978 (CIO)

Today's Church in Today's World, The Lambeth Conference 1978, Preparatory Articles. (CIO, London, 1978)

Believing in the Church, Report of the Doctrine Commission (SPCK, London, 1981)

A Strategy for the Church's Ministry, John Tiller (CIO Publishing, London, 1983)

Women in Training, (ACCM Occasional Paper, No. 14, 1983)

Joint Ministries Consultation (ACCM Occasional Paper, No. 16, 1984)

Ecumenical Reports and Essays

Baptism, Eucharist and Ministry (Faith and Order No. 111, WCC, Geneva, 1982)

The Final Report of the Anglican-Roman Catholic International Commission (CTS/SPCK, London 1982)

God's Reign and Our Unity, The Report of the Anglican-Reformed International Commission 1981–1984. (SPCK, London, The Saint Andrew Press, Edinburgh, 1984)

Pro and Con the Ordination of Women: Report and Papers from the Anglican/Roman Catholic Consultation (Seabury Professional Service, New York, 1976)

Declaration on the Question of the Admission of Women to Ministerial Priesthood Inter Insigniores (CTS, London, 1977)

Towards Visible Unity: Proposals for a Covenant (CCC, London, 1980)
The Failure of the English Covenant (CCC, London, 1982)
Essays on the Covenant (BCC, London)
The Community of Women and Men in the Church, (WCC, Geneva, 1983)

Books, Pamphlets and Periodicals

Man, Woman, and Priesthood, ed. P.C. Moore (SPCK, London, 1978)

Christian Priesthood Examined: Richard Hanson (Lutterworth, Guildford and London, 1979)

Ministry: a case for change, Edward Schillebeeckx (English translation, SCM Press, London, 1981)

Obeying Christ in a changing World: The Lord Christ (Collins, London, 1977)

Feminine in the Church, ed. Monica Furlong (SPCK, London. 1984)

Issues Facing Christians Today, John Stott (Marshall-Pickering, Basingstoke, 1984)

Women and the Priesthood, ed. T. Hopko (St Vladimir's Seminary, New York, 1983)

MAN as Male and Female — A Study in Sexual Relationships from a Theological Point of View, Paul K Jewett, (Eerdmans, Grand Rapids, 1975)

The Ordination of Women, Paul K Jewett, (Eerdmans, Grand Rapids, 1980)

Faith, Feminism and the Christ, Patricia Wilson-Kastner (Fortress Press, Philadelphia, 1983)

Women and Priesthood: Future Directions ed. Carroll Stuhlmueller (Liturgical Press, Collegeville, 1978)

Called to be me, Margaret Cundiff (Triangle, London, 1982)

Following On, Margaret Cundiff (Triangle, London, 1983)

Women in the Priesthood of the Church, E.L. Mascall (Church Union, London, 1958)

Christ and his Bride, John Saward (CLA, London, 1977)

A Fully Human Priesthood, Oliver Tomkins (MOW, London, 1984)

Churchman January 1977, article by Michael Williams; No. 4 1978, article by Colin Craston and Gordon Wenham

Theology, May 1984, article by George Newsom

Epworth Review, January 1984, paper by Graham Leonard

Midstream, July 1984, Paper by Mary Tanner

Ecumenical Review, July 1977, article by Christian Howard